GHOSTS IN THE FOG

The Untold Story of Alaska's WWII Invasion

SAMANTHA SEIPLE

SCHOLASTIC PRESS / NEW YORK

Library of Congress Cataloging-in-Publication Data Available

ISBN 978-0-545-29654-0

10 9 8 7 6 5 4 3 2 1   11 12 13 14 15

Printed in the U.S.A.   23
First edition, October 2011

Designed by Becky Terhune

DEDICATED TO
THE MEN, WOMEN, AND CHILDREN
WHOSE LIVES WERE LOST OR FOREVER
CHANGED BY THE FORGOTTEN WAR.
YOU ARE NOT FORGOTTEN.

CONTENTS

PREFACE
The Forgotten

ON JUNE 7, 1942, Japan invaded Alaska.

On June 10, 1942, the U.S. Navy denied that it happened: "None of our inhabited islands or rocks are troubled with uninvited visitors up to this time."

The Japanese invasion and occupation of the Aleutian Islands in Alaska was shrouded in secrecy. This secrecy was not only for security reasons but also to avoid provoking a widespread panic across the United States and to avoid acknowledging the fact that the westernmost section of Alaska was now part of Japan's quickly expanding empire.

Decades after World War II, the U.S. government kept the documents about the Japanese invasion of Alaska classified, and the Americans who were there when it happened didn't want to talk about it.

Because of this silence, one of the bloodiest and deadliest hand-to-hand combat battles between the United States and Japan was virtually forgotten. This is the story they didn't want you to know.

CHAPTER 1
The Secret in the Dungeon

MAY 14, 1942. PEARL HARBOR, OAHU, HAWAII, FIVE
MONTHS AND ONE WEEK AFTER THE JAPANESE ATTACK.

A soldier stood with a loaded gun in front of a locked steel door. He was guarding the secrets buried below from spies and thieves. No one was allowed to talk about what went on in the "dungeon," and if anyone did, their life was at stake. The armed guard stopped anyone who tried to enter. If necessary, he would shoot to kill.

A tall, thin man with dark hair and glasses was facing the locked steel door. The armed guard didn't bother him. That's because Lieutenant Commander Edwin Layton, known as Eddie to his friends, possessed the security clearance to enter. Plus, he was a regular. The soldier unlocked the door for him and stepped aside.

Eddie rushed down the flight of stairs deep into the dungeon. He stopped when he got to the bottom and stood in front of another locked steel door. As he waited anxiously for it to open, he thought about the urgent phone call he'd received earlier in the day.

"I've got something so hot here it's burning the top of my desk!" said Lieutenant Commander Joseph J. Rochefort.

"What is it?" asked Eddie.

But Joe wouldn't tell Eddie over the phone. Since Joe wasn't one to exaggerate, Eddie immediately stopped what he was doing and rushed over to meet with him.

Eddie and Joe, who were both known for their quick wit and brilliance, became lifelong friends when they met onboard a ship making its way across the Pacific to Japan in 1929. The navy had sent them to Tokyo to learn Japanese. At the time, it was rare for any American to speak Japanese, but it wasn't unusual for the Japanese to be fluent in English.

During their three years in

Lieutenant Commander Edwin Layton

Lieutenant Commander Joseph J. Rochefort

9

Japan, Joe never once mentioned to Eddie that his background involved cryptography, a relatively new field involving cracking codes from intercepted messages. The navy called a cryptanalyst a "cryppy."

Following his three years in Japan, Eddie would find himself back in the United States working in naval intelligence. Using his firsthand knowledge of Japan and by studying detailed maps, Eddie identified strategic targets within Japan's electric power distribution network for the United States to bomb in case of war.

During this time, Eddie was also assigned to naval communications and introduced to code cracking, becoming a cryppy himself. He and Joe would cross paths again in 1936 when they were assigned to the same ship. And, five years later, on May 15, 1941, their paths crossed once more when Joe was assigned to work in the dungeon.

Joe was the head cryppy in the dungeon, located in the basement of the administration building of the Fourteenth Naval District. Being the head cryppy meant that Joe was the commander in charge of the combat intelligence unit, also called Station Hypo.

Station Hypo didn't really describe the group — and this was intentional. The name was a cover

Machine operators inside Station Hypo

to keep their work in the dungeon a secret from everyone. If the enemy ever found out who worked there and captured them, they would be tortured or even killed in an attempt to get top secret information.

Joe oversaw a team of one hundred cryppies, translators, typists, punch card operators, and clerks. Their top secret work involved cracking the Japanese naval traffic codes, specifically the Japanese Navy 25, or JN-25, by intercepting Japanese messages. This was no easy feat.

The navy set up listening posts in China, Guam,

the Philippines, Hawaii, and Washington state. At these posts, radiomen, called roofers, wore headsets and scanned the radio airways. They were listening to intercept the Japanese Morse code messages. The roofers would translate the Japanese Morse code of dots and dashes into Japanese kana characters, which represent the phonetic sounds of the Japanese language. Any secretly coded messages were then sent over a secure cable line or delivered in person by a courier to the cryppies, who tried to convert the kana characters into English. Anything they discovered about the Japanese navy's next plan of attack, Joe reported to Eddie who, in turn, informed Admiral Chester W. Nimitz.

Admiral Chester W. Nimitz

Admiral Nimitz was the commander in chief of the U.S. Pacific Fleet. He needed to know the exact location of the next Japanese attack. The situation was dire.

Since the 1930s, the Japanese had been aggressively expanding their empire, which they called the Greater East Asia Co-Prosperity Sphere. Japan's main motivation was its need for resources, such as oil, rubber, tin, and nickel, for military armaments. To get these, they conquered countries rich in these resources. The Japanese leaders claimed that the resulting economic growth would bring them out of the Great Depression, an economic crash that was plaguing the world.

Although Hirohito, the emperor of Japan, was worshipped as a god, he didn't actually run the country. General Hideki Tojo, who became Japan's prime minister on October 16, 1941, and other military leaders made the decisions and controlled the government.

In fact, Emperor Hirohito opposed the military leaders' decisions but didn't dare voice his opinions. He feared they would turn against him — General Tojo was known to assassinate anyone who stood in his way.

The Japanese military was undefeated and unstoppable. The soldiers were well trained, highly skilled, disciplined, and followed the samurai warrior code of *bushido*, meaning they valued honor before their lives and would fight to the death. To a Japanese soldier, it was extremely shameful to surrender, and those who did were tortured and executed.

Japan wanted to be a world power and rule all of East Asia and the Pacific. In 1940, Japan formed an alliance with Germany's Adolf Hitler and Italy's Benito Mussolini, who were leading wars to expand their own empires in Europe and North Africa. The alliance was called the Rome-Berlin-Tokyo Axis. Hitler promised the Japanese everlasting domination in the Pacific region — including the west coast of North, South, and Central America — if they went to war.

On December 7, 1941, Admiral Isoroku Yamamoto, commander in chief of Japan's Imperial Fleet, masterminded the surprise attack on Pearl Harbor. During the two-hour bombing, 2,343 American soldiers were killed and 1,272 were wounded. The Japanese sank four American battleships, and of the 394 aircraft, 188 were destroyed and 150 were severely damaged. Japan successfully brought the U.S. Pacific Fleet to its knees and brought America into World War II.

With the United States weakened and unable to stop the Japanese in the Pacific, it only took the Japanese six months to quickly and easily conquer

Guam, Indochina (now parts of Laos and Vietnam), Thailand, Wake Island, Hong Kong, Manila, Singapore, Malaya, Java, and Burma (now Myanmar).

Admiral Isoroku Yamamoto

Admiral Yamamoto needed to act fast before the United States had time to recover and gain strength. His strategic plan was to spur the Pacific Fleet into battle and annihilate it.

With only three battleships left, Admiral Nimitz's resources were low, and the stakes were incredibly high. If he made one wrong decision, the United States could lose the war with Japan.

Joe Rochefort and his team were frantically trying to find out where the next strike would be so that Admiral Nimitz could ambush the enemy and turn the odds to favor the United States.

Back in the dungeon on that day in May, the steel door opened, and Eddie walked into the cold, windowless room. The air conditioner was blasting to prevent a meltdown. The dungeon was a cutting-edge, high-tech operation of key punchers, collators, and machine tabulators.

The team received five hundred to a thousand intercepted messages each day. For each hundred-word message, two hundred punch cards were made. A punch card is made with a machine that looks like a typewriter. Each key on the typewriter-like machine corresponds to a letter or number. When the key is hit, a hole is punched into a card that represents that particular letter or number. By the end of April, the team had used two to three million punch cards. The desks and floor were overflowing with stacks of papers because there was no time to organize and file them, but Joe was a walking encyclopedia of information.

"I could remember back maybe three or four months," said Joe. "Everything was in my head. Eventually, of course, you've got to get away from this. You've got to get organized. But we didn't have time to get organized."

Like most cryppies, Joe was a natural at solving crossword puzzles. He also loved playing bridge, a trick-taking card game that requires tactics, probability, communication, and memory.

"If you desire to be a really great cryptanalyst, being a little bit nuts helps," said Joe. "A cryptanalyst from those that I have observed is usually an odd character."

But, of course, Joe didn't consider it odd that he wore a reddish smoking jacket over his navy uniform and slippers on his feet. To Joe, it was perfectly logical. The smoking jacket kept him warm, and his slippers were comfortable.

It was typical for Joe to work a twenty-two-hour shift before taking a break, but he wouldn't go home to sleep. Joe only went home "when someone told me I ought to take a bath." Instead, he would stretch out and nap on one of the cots set up in a corner of the dungeon.

"An intelligence officer has one task, one job, one mission," said Joe. "This is to tell his commander, his superior, today, what the Japanese are going to do tomorrow. This is his job. If he doesn't do this, then he's failed."

When the Japanese shocked the Americans by sailing across the Pacific undetected with their battle fleet and bombing Pearl Harbor, Joe felt he'd failed in his mission.

"I felt very guilty that I didn't know what was up on December 6. I should have, but I just hadn't enough time or personnel," said Joe.

Cracking codes wasn't an easy job and Joe had a stomach ulcer to prove it.

"It wasn't that we could read their [the Japanese]

transmissions like we could a newspaper," said Joe. "We'd find clues to a new message buried in some old message. That's why the place always looked in such a mess. We were always pawing through old messages."

The JN-25 code had forty-five thousand groups of five digits, each of which represented a Japanese word. A Japanese word or idea is represented by a picture that contains one to thirty strokes.

A major difficulty for the American codebreakers was homonyms. A homonym is a word that has more than one meaning. In English, *bear* is a homonym. *Bear* can mean to carry or it can refer to the shaggy-haired wild animal. In Japanese, the word *seiko* means watch, success, starlight, perfume, and it has more than a dozen other meanings. There are thousands of homonyms in the Japanese language.

To further boggle the minds of code crackers, random numbers were thrown into the mix to increase the level of difficulty of deciphering the message.

After spending hours trying to decipher an intercepted message, some parts were still too difficult to crack, and blanks would remain. An example of a partially deciphered message that Joe's cryppies worked on looked like this:

Tommy Dyer, one of the cryppies, at work cracking codes

STRIKING FORCE OPERATIONS ORDER 6.
Commander Destroyers STRIKING FORCE,
will assign 4 destroyers (for each group?) to
screen the below units en route _____:
A. AKAGI
B. HIRYU, HIRI, KONGO
Change screening (orders) for
SORYU and KIRISHIMA.
Each ship of below units report date when
they will in all respects be ready for sea.

When the cryppy couldn't crack any more of
the code, he would hand it off to Joe, who would
try to figure out any blanks that were left in the

message. He would review and fill in the blanks of an estimated 140 messages a day.

On May 14, 1942, when Joe read the Japanese words *koryaku butai,* meaning "invasion force," in a partially decrypted message, followed by the letters *AF,* he made a quick deduction. He called Eddie and told him to hurry to the dungeon. Joe knew AF was an island air base, and he had a hunch it was Midway — a U. S. territory northwest of Honolulu in the Pacific Ocean.

Eddie left the dungeon to immediately inform Admiral Nimitz. "From that afternoon on," said Eddie, "despite all that has been written, there was never any doubt in Nimitz's mind that Midway was the main objective of the Japanese operation."

But other people weren't convinced.

"Oh, it was quite a scene," said Joe. "The Australians were telling us the Japanese were going to come after them. The army was telling us the Japanese were going after San Francisco. I told them the target would be Midway."

Over the next five days, Joe hatched a plan to prove his hunch was right. Joe's assistant, Lieutenant Commander Jasper Holmes, told him the island of Midway depended on a facility to supply fresh drinking water. On May 19, 1942, Joe asked Admiral Nimitz to order an uncoded message be sent in plain English stating that the facility was broken and Midway needed a supply of fresh water delivered quickly.

As suspected, the Japanese intercepted the message, and on that same day, the Japanese intelligence unit on Wake Island sent a message to Tokyo informing them that AF was short of fresh water. The Americans intercepted the message and it confirmed, without a doubt, that AF was Midway. But the cryppies' work wasn't finished. They still didn't know the specifics, such as when it was going to happen.

As luck would have it, on May 20, 1942, Admiral Yamamoto sent a ciphered message that laid out the details of the entire Japanese operation. The U.S. naval intelligence intercepted it, and Joe and his team worked around the clock cracking it.

Five days later, on May 25, 1942, 90 percent of the message was deciphered, and Joe delivered the information directly to Admiral Nimitz. Joe knew the details of Japan's next plan of attack — and the Japanese weren't just going to bomb and obliterate the U.S. forces on Midway.

They would first attack the Aleutian Islands, the thousand-mile chain of volcanic islands that extend from the tip of the Alaskan Peninsula to the Russian Komandorski Islands.

The Japanese planned to bomb the largest community in the Aleutians, Dutch Harbor, where Fort Mears army base and the Dutch Harbor naval operating base were also located. These two military installations were the only defenses in the Aleutian Islands.

The Japanese strategized that the bombing raid on Dutch Harbor would divert Admiral Nimitz's attention and draw his fleet away to the north, leaving Midway wide open for bombings and an invasion. After the raid, they planned to invade and occupy two islands at the western end of the Aleutian chain, Attu and Kiska, giving them a toehold in Alaska.

Admiral Nimitz was forced to make a dire decision: How would he defend Midway and the Aleutians against Japan's immense fleet with a battered and weakened Pacific Fleet?

Basing his decision solely on the cryppies' intelligence, Admiral Nimitz took a huge risk. He sent his entire carrier fleet to Midway to battle it out with the Japanese, but he also sent Rear Admiral

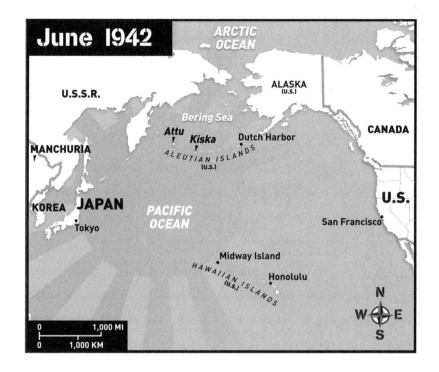

June 1942

ARCTIC OCEAN

U.S.S.R.

ALASKA (U.S.)

Bering Sea

Attu Kiska Dutch Harbor

ALEUTIAN ISLANDS (U.S.)

CANADA

MANCHURIA

KOREA JAPAN

PACIFIC OCEAN

Tokyo

U.S.

San Francisco

Midway Island

HAWAIIAN ISLANDS (U.S.)

Honolulu

N
W E
S

0   1,000 MI
0   1,000 KM

Robert A. Theobald to command a small fleet in the Aleutians.

Admiral Theobald's mission was to defend the Aleutians from the Japanese invasion. But he didn't. Instead, he made a fatal mistake that would end his career.

Theobald chalked up the decrypted messages as guesswork, and he assumed Admiral Yamamoto was trying to trick him by sending a fake message outlining a phony strategic plan. Theobald strategized that the Japanese were trying to lure his naval forces to the western Aleutians, where they

23

would be trapped and destroyed. So he ignored the intelligence when he outlined his plan of operation.

He based his plan on the theory that the real Japanese plan was to first attack the Alaskan army airfield bases Fort Glenn on Umnak Island and Fort Randall at Cold Bay, which had been built to provide air protection for the Dutch Harbor naval base. When the two bases had been seized, the Japanese would attack Dutch Harbor. After the Japanese gained control of Dutch Harbor, they would be in a position to launch an attack on the Kodiak Island– Kenai Peninsula area, which would position them to launch air attacks on the mainland of Alaska as well as Seattle, San Francisco, and Vancouver, British Columbia, in Canada. As a result, Theobald planned on ambushing the Japanese four hundred miles south of Kodiak Island, which is a thousand miles *east* of the Aleutians.

So while Midway would mark a turning point in the war for the United States and be celebrated as a victory, the same wasn't true for the Aleutians.

They were about to be dealt a deadly and devastating blow.

CHAPTER 2
Invasion of the Ghost Warriors

It was an unusually sunny and windless day when a quiet stillness descended on the village of Attu in the Aleutian Islands. It lingered with an unshakable persistence like the thin ring of fog that clung to

Village of Attu

the foot of the rugged mountains. But this stillness wasn't calming. It was menacing.

As Mike Lokanin walked over the wooden sidewalks that covered the slippery mud, a nagging dread kept clouding his thoughts, and sometimes his heart thumped so hard he felt like he was choking.

When he looked around the island, which was located on the westernmost tip of the Aleutian chain, everything appeared beautiful to him. The mountains were a lush green. Wildflowers were sprouting and beginning to bloom. As he gazed at Chichagof Harbor, the island looked like it was sitting on top of the ocean.

Mike was seven years old the first time he laid eyes on Attu. That was twenty-three years ago, in 1919. It was the same year the deadly Spanish flu swept through Alaska and killed his parents.

It was also the year Mike first met Alfred Somerville, captain and owner of the trading schooner *Emma*. They met when Captain Somerville brought some medicine for Mike's dad. This first meeting led to events that would change Mike's life, forever sealing his fate.

After his parents' deaths, orphaned and with no one to take care of him, Mike came onboard

Mike Lokanin (front in sailor's hat) with Attu natives

Captain Somerville's trading schooner even though he wasn't sure where they were headed. Captain Somerville took Mike under his wing.

They sailed one thousand miles away from Unalaska, Mike's hometown. Then one morning when Mike woke up, everything was quiet. He got out of bed and went to the deck to take a look.

The first thing Mike saw when he looked out on the calm Chichagof Harbor in Attu was a skin boat with two men paddling toward the schooner.

Before the canoelike dory became the boat of choice among the Aleuts, the skin boat predominated. The skin boat, also called a *baidarka*, was a kayak covered in sea lion skins. The *baidarka* was built using driftwood, and it contained one to three openings where people sat, one behind the other. The boat was propelled using a double-bladed paddle.

The Aleuts were extraordinary kayakers. They learned from an early age how to handle the skin boat in the wild and stormy sea. They were able to navigate by feeling the direction of the currents under their kayaks and the wind on their faces. They were so adept that they could kayak through blinding fog and in the darkness of night without losing their way.

They used their *baidarkas* to hunt for food in the ocean. Power and precision were required, which wasn't easy to achieve in the rough and choppy open waters. Before the advent of guns, the Aleuts used a throwing board to hunt, which they called an *atl-atl*, in order to improve their speed and distance.

The *atl-atl* is a wooden board that is about a foot and a half long, depending on its owner's hand size, that catapults darts and harpoons. One side of it is painted red, to lure the sea otter into striking distance, and the other side is painted black.

When the men spotted a sea otter, they would

form a circle around it. They aimed their darts at the sea otter's head because they didn't want to tear its fur. Once the sea otter was hit with a dart, the hunter raised the throwing board and showed the black side to the other hunters. This was a signal of success and symbolized the color of the sea otter's fur. The hunter whose dart was the closest to the sea otter's snout was credited with the kill.

The Aleuts were expert fishermen and also hunted sea lions, fur seals, and walruses. In the eastern part of the Aleutians, certain men were chosen to hunt whales.

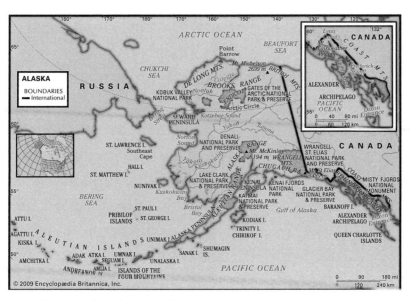

Map showing the Aleutian Islands

Whale hunting was a dangerous and prestigious profession, and many hunters died young. Usually, the father was a whale hunter and his skills were passed on to the son. They used a special poison on their spears, and when the whale was struck, they waited for it to drift ashore.

While standing on the bow of the schooner, seven-year-old Mike looked past the skin boats to the village of Attu. Salmon were hanging out to dry just outside the *barabaras*. These sod homes were built partially into the ground, and they provided shelter from the fierce storms and hurricane force winds called *williwaws*, which sound like a train roaring overhead. *Williwaws* plague the Aleutians all year long.

The Aleutians are synonymous with relentless bad weather. A semipermanent low pressure system, called the Aleutian Low, hovers over the Aleutian Islands. Cyclonic disturbances form when moist warm air, called the Japanese Current, flows from the tropics and collides with the cold air from the Arctic, spawning thick, icy fog and violent storms. As the Earth rotates, these storms move from west to east, affecting the weather in Alaska and the Pacific Northwest.

When Mike finally went ashore that day, the sand felt like powder on his bare feet.

Captain Somerville co-owned a fox fur farm and managed

Attuan boys with Arctic blue foxes

the trading post on Attu. Trading posts were part of the Alaska Commercial Company, and they dated back to 1776. That was when Catherine the Great, the empress of Russia who also ruled Alaska, granted the company's trading rights.

Trading posts were set up throughout Alaska, and people traded furs, gold, walrus tusks, handwoven baskets, and other valuables for store-bought merchandise. Cash was seldom used. In the Aleutians, people relied on the trading posts for luxuries such as coal, lumber, flour, sugar, tea, and tobacco, to name a few.

Mike lived on Attu with Captain Somerville for four years, until the captain moved back to Unalaska. Mike chose to stay in Attu, and Attu chief Mike Hodikoff and his wife, Anecia, adopted him, happily making him a part of their family.

Chief Mike Hodikoff (left) and his son, George

But today, nineteen years later, Mike couldn't shake his feeling of doom, even as he made his way through the picturesque village of Attu, which he and forty-three others called home. As he passed the nine wooden cottages that had replaced the *barabaras,* he could smell the salmon cooking for dinner as its aroma wafted through the smoky stovepipe. Mike could hear the rhythmic sound of the gas motors in the power plant that gave electricity to the nearby schoolhouse.

When he saw his neighbor John Golodoff, he smiled warmly and stopped to talk with him.

"Are you going out with your father tomorrow?" said Mike in the Aleut language.

Although most Aleuts could speak English and many spoke Russian, too, the Aleut language was their mother tongue, which had three different dialects depending on where in the Aleutian Islands you lived. English was taught as a second language in school.

"I will be out tomorrow if the weather keeps like this," said John.

Even though the Attuans' cottages were well maintained and most had the modern convenience of running water, none had electricity or refrigerators. They used cellars to store dried and salted meat, and the Attuans regularly hunted, fished, and gathered fresh food.

June was the perfect time of the year to find seagull eggs. Their nests could be found on grassy hillsides and on sea cliffs. The Aleuts fearlessly climbed the steep and jagged cliffs or dangled from a rope to collect eggs to cook and eat.

Birds are plentiful in the Aleutians, with over five million flying around and roosting. Besides seagulls and ducks, there are puffins, storm petrels, ravens, sanderlings, sand pipers, bald eagles, geese, albatross, auklets, and murres. During the summer, all through the day and night, the birds can be heard calling out to one another as they sit on their eggs or care for their newly hatched chicks.

Surprisingly, however, the Aleutian Islands are treeless. This is a mystery that continues to puzzle scientists because the soil is rich and there are remains of a forest, which proves that at some point in time, trees flourished.

Since the Aleutians are treeless, wood is scarce. Lumber was imported, but the Aleuts also collected driftwood for their homes, boats, and tools. Because of this, they didn't like to burn wood for fuel. Instead, they preferred to burn seal blubber in their lanterns and stoves.

As the sun shifted behind the mountain, a shadow fell on the bay, and Mike said good-bye to John. Before Mike went home to his wife and daughter, he saw Foster Jones come out of the small building that housed the power plant.

Foster and his wife, Etta, lived in a cabin by the schoolhouse on Attu. They had moved to Attu in August 1941. Both worked for the Bureau of Indian Affairs (BIA), the federal government agency

Foster and his wife, Etta Jones

created to protect the welfare of American Indians and Alaskan natives, including the Aleuts and Inuits (also known as Eskimos). The BIA's services included managing the school system, and this involved sending teachers to the villages.

Etta, who grew up in Connecticut, was Attu's schoolteacher and nurse, and Foster, who was originally from Ohio, was Attu's radio operator.

Since there were no phones on the island, the radio was the only communication link to the outside world. It was Foster's job to send weather reports four times a day to the naval radio station 770 miles away in Dutch Harbor, and this two-

Attu schoolhouse

way radio communication was how he learned that the Japanese had bombed the navy and army installations at Dutch Harbor on Amaknak Island just three days ago.

It was also Foster's job to report any sightings of Japanese ships. If anyone saw one, Foster was to use the code words, "The boys went out today but didn't see a boat. They came home and went to eat fried codfish."

But so far, no one on Attu had seen any.

The only report Foster made was to the Bureau of Indian Affairs. He told them that every day on the radio he heard Tokyo Rose, a Japanese radio announcer known for spreading propaganda, say, "Attu, we are coming."

Just a few weeks ago in May, the navy had tried unsuccessfully to evacuate Attu. The choppy sea and stormy weather made it too dangerous and difficult. The navy promised to come back for them. No one knew when that would be, but everyone on Attu had packed their belongings. They were ready and waiting.

Early the next morning, on June 7, 1942, a ship was spotted just outside the harbor. At first, it was hard to tell through the heavy fog if the ship was

American or Japanese. There weren't any flags flying to give an indication.

"We had noticed the big ship anchored outside the harbor," said Etta. "But, of course, had thought it was our own."

When the ship finally raised its flag, there was no mistaking it — the red rising sun against the white background. Their worst nightmare had come true. The Japanese soldiers had arrived.

"On Sunday morning [June 7] a little after eleven we were all coming out of church when we saw them [the Japanese] coming out of the hills. So many of them," said Attuan Innokenty Golodoff. "Twenty came down. We had no knives, no guns, no nothing. The batch had no boss. They were young and they shot up the village. They hit Anna Hodikoff [Chief Mike Hodikoff's sister-in-law] in the leg. The second bunch came and told them to stop. I saw one of their own men dead by the schoolhouse. They must have shot him."

At first, the Attuans wanted to grab their rifles and fire back.

"Do not shoot," said Chief Hodikoff. "Maybe the Americans can save us yet."

While the Japanese soldiers fired bullets through

the windows and walls of their home, Foster Jones sat at his radio and transmitted a message to the navy listening post in Dutch Harbor that the Japanese were attacking. Etta threw all of their letters and reports into the fire that was burning in their fireplace. When the bullets died down, Foster went outside their home and surrendered to the Japanese.

A Japanese soldier stormed past Foster and held a bayonet against Etta's stomach.

"How many have you here?" demanded the Japanese officer.

"Two," said Etta. "How many have you?"

"Two thousand," he said.

The Japanese soldiers quickly rounded up the Attuans and herded them into the schoolhouse.

When Mike walked into the schoolhouse, he said hello to Foster, but a Japanese guard ordered him not to speak.

"Well, Mike," said Foster, disobeying the guard. "The world has seemed to change today. We are under Japanese rule now."

At that moment another Japanese guard came into the schoolhouse with the American flag. A Japanese flag now flew in its place.

A proclamation in Japanese was read by a military police (MP) officer, and a Japanese interpreter named Karl Kaoru Kasukabe translated it into English for them.

"An officer showed us how to bow to the emperor and also to the Jap[anese] commander," said Etta. "Mimeographed sheets were distributed to all of us, which gave the rules of occupation. The natives, the sheet said, were to be freed from United States 'tyranny.' No harm was intended, and we were to go ahead with our way of life as if nothing had happened. But we were to pay strict attention to any orders issued by the Jap[anese] commander."

What the people of Attu didn't know was that the Japanese interpreter, Karl Kasukabe, had spent his childhood in the United States, where his sister, Mary, and his father still lived. His father had helped build the U.S. railroads and was now a farmer in Pocatello, Idaho, a small town.

When Karl was a teenager, his mother abruptly pulled him out of school and took him and his sister and brothers back to Japan. She was upset about the "democratic education" Karl was receiving in America. His parents viewed democracy as having the freedom to do what you want. They wanted Karl to have a "monarchy education" in Japan, where children learned to be loyal to the emperor, dutiful to their parents, and obedient to and unquestioning of authority.

His parents would soon find out that it was too late for their eldest son. When Karl was enrolled in a Japanese high school, the military officer assigned to the school deemed Karl "an undesirable student" because of Karl's democratic and liberal ideas. The military officer punished Karl by disqualifying his military drilling credit, effectively denying him a college education and regular employment.

Through sheer grit and hard work, Karl managed to become qualified as a first class military interpreter in English and a second class military interpreter in Russian. He also maintained a job in the Mitsubishi factory where the infamous Zero fighter plane was manufactured. When the Japanese went to war with America, Karl's job as an interpreter brought him to Attu.

After Karl finished translating the proclamation and a speech from the officer in command, none of the captured Americans said a word. With the exception of Foster and Etta, the Japanese told the Attuans that they could leave and go home. It was nine o'clock at night, and no one had eaten or had anything to drink all day. They found their homes looted and pockmarked with bullet holes.

Just as Mike was sitting down to have some tea with his wife, Parascovia, and baby daughter, Titiana, a Japanese soldier came in and ordered Mike to come with him.

Mike and his neighbor, Alex Prossoff, were taken back to the schoolhouse, where Karl was waiting for them and carrying a sword. Karl warned Mike and Alex not to speak to the Joneses, and he ordered them to help Foster and Etta move their possessions out of their nearby cabin. The Japanese soldiers would now be living in the Joneses' home.

While gathering their things, Foster and Etta tried to take some food with them. This angered Karl.

"I was beaten with the butt end of a rifle and struck across the back by a Jap[anese] soldier who had been acting as an interpreter," said Etta. "He knocked me down, stepped on me, and kicked me in the stomach. Then I saw him hit my husband and knock him down."

Karl slapped Foster on the face, knocked him down, and kicked him. Then Karl picked him up, slapped him, knocked him down again, and kicked him out the door.

Mike couldn't stop shaking as he and Alex helped

carry Foster and Etta's things to an abandoned house. On the way, he found a shoe that belonged to Etta stuck in the mud. Afterward, Mike ran home. He stood outside the door to his house for a few minutes, trying to calm his uncontrollable shaking.

"I didn't want to scare my wife," said Mike. He couldn't help but think that if it happened to Etta and Foster Jones, it could also happen to him and his family.

That night Mike barely slept. There was constant noise from the firing of Japanese machine guns.

Early the next morning, Japanese soldiers came and took Foster away. They believed he was an American spy, working in conjunction with the Russians. Russia was only 765 miles away and an ally of the United States. The Japanese feared that the Russians would attack them while they occupied the Aleutians, and this threatened their plans to expand Japan's empire.

Hours later the Japanese guards came for Etta. They took her to a room where she saw the body of her dead husband. Shocked and horrified, Etta could barely stand up as they marshaled her back to her room.

Soon after, Karl came to Mike's door.

"Mr. Foster Jones is dead," he said to Mike.

He ordered Mike to come with him to the house where Foster's body lay. It was there that Mike met another interpreter, named Mr. Imai.

"He said Foster cut his own wrist with his pocketknife," said Mike.

Mike thought it was strange that after the Japanese captured Foster they would allow him to keep his pocketknife, but he kept his thoughts to himself.

Karl and Mr. Imai called Mike into the room, where he saw Foster's dead body.

"He was wrapped in a blanket," said Mike. "They told me to bury him without a coffin. So I dug a grave by our church."

Later, Mike whispered to Etta that he had buried Foster near the church.

A few days later, Etta was ordered to board a Japanese ship. Before she left, Karl Kasukabe stopped her.

"He shook my hand," said Etta, "and apologized, and said he was following the commander's orders."

That was one of Etta's last memories of her life in Attu.

The Attuans would not see Etta Jones again.

For the next three months, the Japanese lived with the Attuans on the island. Just a single strand of barbed wire was needed to keep the Attuans fenced in, because not only were there Japanese soldiers standing guard, but their camp also surrounded the village.

"They guarded our houses all the time," said Innokenty. "We could go outside for fresh air but not away from the houses."

The Attuans did not have much food, and they were forced to tear boards off their homes to burn for fuel.

The Japanese did allow them to occasionally go out and fish for food, but they were always accompanied by the Japanese interpreter, Mr. Imai, and they were required to fly little Japanese flags on their boat.

The ocean was filled with halibut, cod, salmon, poggy fish, and herring, and at low tide there was an abundance of clams and sea urchins. When the Attuans went out, they caught a lot of fish, but the Japanese made sure they remained hungry.

"The Japanese took most of our fish away," said Mike. "We didn't have enough fish for the whole village. All I had was one codfish left for myself."

On September 14, 1942, a Japanese coal carrier arrived. The Attuans were told to pack their things — they were being sent to Japan.

"We tell them we didn't want to go," said Innokenty. "But they tell us we must go to Japan and promise us they will take us home again when the war is over."

Mr. Imai kindly told them to pack as much food as they could because it would be scarce in Japan.

"So each family takes flour, sugar, barrels of salt fish," said Mike. "We don't know how we are going to live in Japan. So we take tents, stoves, fishnets, windows, and doors."

"Everything except our homes," said Innokenty.

It was after midnight when the Attuans went onboard the ship. The children were crying because they didn't want to leave, but the Japanese soldiers picked them up and forced them down below with the others into the dark and stifling hold, where the coal had been stored.

"Everything was black and dirty," said Mike.

What they didn't know at the time was that this was a death sentence.

CHAPTER 3
The Rising Storm

JULY 26, 1942. KISKA, ALASKA, FORTY-NINE DAYS AFTER
THE JAPANESE INVADED ALASKA.

On the northwest coast of Kiska Island, Alaska, at Conquer Point, down a treacherously steep ravine of jagged volcanic rocks, a man with unkempt brown hair and a thick beard sat near a creek. He was desperately trying to write his name on his hunting jacket. It wasn't an easy task.

The biting wind deadened his hand, making it difficult to grasp the dull pencil, which was all he had to write with. For a time, he had marked each day off by carving a notch up the side of the pencil, but somewhere along the way he had lost count. One thing he knew for certain, though, was that he was starving.

Every morning, as the morning fog clung to him, soaking his clothes and chilling his bones, but, more importantly, keeping him hidden from plain sight, he dared to venture out of the cave where he slept. He trekked down the rocky ravine in his rubber-soled boots to the creek, where he dipped the hood of his jacket into the ice-cold water for a drink.

Today, however, something unexpected happened. As he was walking to the creek, he suddenly fainted. When he finally regained consciousness, he knew he had a life-or-death decision to make. But first he needed to write his name on his jacket.

His canvas hunting jacket was tattered now and didn't keep him warm in the wet, windy, and foggy Aleutian weather, but he was forced to make do with what little he had. When he finally finished writing out his full name, he looked it over to make sure it was legible. It read: WILLIAM CHARLES HOUSE.

He actually went by the name Charlie, but it was important that his entire name was clearly written. This way when his dead body was found, it would be easy to identify him.

It had been sixty-nine days since Charlie had first arrived on Kiska on May 18, 1942, and it was the luck of the draw that the navy assigned him there. Charlie was an aerographer's mate first class, also known as an aerologist or weatherman. On

Kiska, he was in charge of the weather team that was made up of nine other men and one mascot, their dog. The weather station on Kiska was to be one of four weather stations set up on the Aleutian Islands during World War II. The others were to be located on Atka, Attu, and Kanaga.

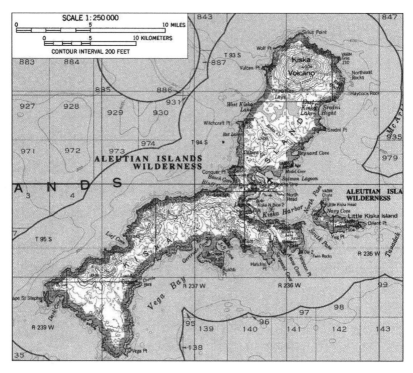

Map of Kiska

The four men who would lead the weather teams randomly picked their assigned location by drawing slips of paper out of a hat. Charlie happened to pick Atka, but when fellow aerographer Ed Hudson asked him to switch and go to Kiska, Charlie agreed. At the time, no one suspected the life-threatening ordeal that was about to descend on Charlie and his weather team.

It was imperative for the military to set up weather stations in the Aleutians. The weather was top secret information. During the war in the Pacific, the weather reports from the Aleutians were crucial to strategic military operations. The weather forecast determined when the military would attack the enemy. Since weather systems move from west to east, the Japanese knew what the weather was like before the Americans, and they used it to their advantage. When Japan attacked Pearl Harbor, the Japanese military hid their fleet behind a storm front that was heading east toward Hawaii. This strategy allowed the Japanese fleet to remain undetected by American scouting planes and ships.

After the attack on Pearl Harbor, the ships in the Pacific maintained radio silence so the enemy would not know their location and bomb them. Since the U.S. military could no longer rely on these ships for daily weather reports, their attention turned to the Aleutians because these islands are the westernmost part of the United States.

However, the weather was difficult to predict in

the Aleutians and was accurate only 60 percent of the time, because the cold air from the Arctic clashed with the warm air from the Pacific, creating the sudden and violent *williwaws*. Also contributing to the difficulty in predicting the weather were the weather instruments available at the time. Unlike today, during World War II, there were no meteorological satellites circling the earth, feeding weather data into computers, and creating weather forecast models, which, in turn, make such accurate weather predictions that the computer can pinpoint the time of day it will start to rain.

Pilots gathering in the weather station before taking off from Dutch Harbor

Instead, they relied on people like Charlie and his weather team who read instruments, took measurements, made observations, coded the results, sent the ciphers over the radio, deciphered incoming codes, and mapped and shared their weather information with other weather stations. The weather teams had specific codes for various weather conditions and they used these weather codes to communicate with one another. They used a secret radio transmission code book that was given to them each month to cipher and decipher the weather codes. The ciphered weather reports were transmitted at scheduled times, several times a day, at weather stations set up all over the world.

The weather teams used several instruments to take surface weather readings, such as a thermometer to check the temperature, a barometer to check the air pressure (low pressure means bad weather), an anemometer to measure wind speed and direction, and a rain gauge. They also studied aerology, the branch of meteorology that pays particular attention to the upper atmosphere because this is where the weather changes occur before they are evident on the surface below. Some aerographers also used robot weather balloons to make weather observations in the upper atmosphere.

Aerologists used this information to make predictions of the wind direction and velocity before it occurred at various altitudes. Airplane pilots relied on this information, as did the navy's underwater and aircraft carrier operations, since an aerographer could forecast the surf conditions and determine how the wind would affect the surface waves. If the aerologist reported that the surf was high and the waves were rough, then an underwater attack would not be planned for that day.

But Charlie and his weather team didn't use weather balloons. Instead, they were working on a top secret mission. To this day, the weather team's exact mission is still a secret, but it is believed it had something to do with the antennas they were installing on Kiska and possibly radar, which was an emerging technology. Nevertheless, what is known for certain is that keeping their mission secret from the enemy would cost them dearly.

When Charlie and his nine-man weather team were dropped off at Kiska, they occupied three shacks with electricity and heating supplied by aboveground oil tanks. The shacks were interconnected by wooden sidewalks.

The powerhouse was in the middle, and it contained the electrical generator and weather laboratory with all of the weather measuring instruments. The aerographers slept here in iron bunk beds.

The cookhouse was on one side, and it had a stove and a walk-in refrigerator that stored their six-month supply of food, which included half a cow. Meals were served there twice a day by the cook and his assistant, who slept there.

The third building was the radio shack, from which the radiomen sent the coded weather reports to the navy command in Dutch Harbor. They also slept here.

No one else lived on the 110-square-mile island. The closest village was on Attu, which was 180 miles northwest, and the only time the Aleuts came to Kiska was during hunting season when they trapped blue foxes.

The weather team was isolated and alone with the exception of a sociable and intelligent two-year-old black-and-white shorthaired shepherd dog named Explosion. Explosion got his name when he was born during an accidental dynamite explosion at Dutch Harbor. He was the runt of the litter, and Ensign William C. Jones brought Explosion to Kiska when he helped the weather team install the radio station. Before he left, he gave them Explosion as a mascot.

Explosion was everybody's friend, and he was allowed complete freedom on Kiska. He would roam the area and run in and out of the three shacks whenever he pleased, and he always enjoyed a

Kiska weather team: Front row (left to right): John McCandless, Robert Christensen, Walter Winfrey (holding Explosion), Gilbert Palmer, and Wilford Gaffey. Back row (left to right): James Turner, Rolland Coffield, Charlie House, Lt. Mulls (not present at the time of the attack), Lethayer Eckles, Lou Yaconelli (not present at the time of the attack), and Madison Courtenay

good game of fetch. Explosion also liked to follow the team around while they worked. When it came to bedtime, Explosion slept beside whoever threw a blanket on the floor for him.

Kiska was supposed to be the weather team's home for several years. But then something happened on May 24, 1942, that would change everything. Just six days after Charlie first arrived on Kiska, he saw a plane fly overhead.

Although everyone was trained to spot enemy airplanes, they weren't always easy to recognize, especially when the Japanese painted their planes to look like American ones. So the silhouette of the plane was used to spot the specific characteristics, such as the wingspan, the shape of the wings, the look of the nose, the shape of the fuselage, the shape of the tail, and the profile of the cockpit.

After studying the silhouette, the weather team checked the *Enemy Plane Identification Book*. It was definitely a Japanese plane, specifically a Type 97, Yokosuka reconnaissance seaplane, code name Glen.

They immediately radioed Dutch Harbor with the news, but Charlie was unprepared for their response. The Dutch Harbor radio operator asked

Charlie if he was sure he'd really seen an airplane. Charlie thought it was a ridiculous question and didn't bother to reply.

Instead, the weather team began to work feverishly, preparing for a possible attack. Since they were on their own and basically defenseless, they started to dig zigzag trenches to shield themselves against bombs and machine-gun fire. Hidden away from their main camp, they pitched tents and stashed food and ammunition in case their three shacks were destroyed.

Ten days later, Charlie awoke to the radioman screaming, "Attack! Attack! Attack!" He was spreading the news that the Japanese had bombed Dutch Harbor the day before, on June 3, 1942. The weather team tried and tried to radio Dutch Harbor for more information, but they couldn't get through.

After three nights of sleeping fitfully in their clothes with their guns by their sides and calculating the position of the Japanese fleet using a ten-knot speed, they assumed it was a safe bet that the Japanese weren't anywhere near Kiska. Everyone felt a sense of relief and looked forward to some much-needed sleep.

That night Charlie undressed and fell fast asleep

in the lower bunk. It was around two A.M. on June 7, 1942, when he was startled awake.

"Attack! Attack!" Walter Winfrey screamed from the top bunk.

"Go back to sleep and quit your yelling," Charlie said. "It's not time to get up. You're just having a bad dream."

Walter turned on the lights. "Then what am I doing with this bullet hole in my leg?"

Charlie looked at the machine-gun bullet hole in Walter's right leg. He was wide awake now as the *rat-a-tat* of machine guns shattered the glass windows. They dropped to the floor and dressed quickly. At the sound of the guns firing, Explosion the dog started barking wildly. Charlie pulled on his boots and slipped on his hunting jacket as bullets continued to tear through the shacks.

From the bedroom, they hurried into the aerological room, where they found aerographer James Turner turning the stove on high heat. He and Charlie wasted no time burning the top secret code books.

"Do you have the weather ciphers?" Walter shouted to James.

"No!"

Dodging bullets, Walter crawled under the machine-gun fire and grabbed the weather ciphers. He threw them to James. The top secret ciphers were thrown into the fire.

Meanwhile, a bullet ripped clean through radioman Madison Courtenay's hand when he turned on the transmitter to send a report announcing the Japanese were invading Kiska. Since it would take five minutes for the transmitter to warm up, Madison ran into the bedroom to make sure everyone was awake. As he tried to get back to the transmitter, he became trapped by machine-gun fire. It was impossible to send the report, and the transmitter was quickly shot full of bullets and destroyed by the Japanese machine guns.

When the code books and ciphers were finally burned to ashes, James grabbed his rifle and crawled outside behind the radio shack. Suddenly, the machine guns stopped firing. Charlie grabbed two gray blankets and ran out the door. At first, they couldn't see anything.

What the weather team couldn't see was Captain Takeji Ono of the Japanese Special Naval Landing Force and his 1,250 Japanese soldiers. They had arrived at Kiska about an hour ago and 3,750 more Japanese troops were on their way.

The weather team and Explosion took cover behind a pile of lumber behind the cook shack, but the other shacks were blocking their view of the enemy's whereabouts. They quickly decided to run up a ravine west of the three shacks to where large rocks and low clouds would give them cover.

But as they ran up the hill, flaming tracer bullets the size of baseballs were fired at them, forcing them to drop to the ground. When the coast looked clear, they would get up, run, and dodge more flaming tracer bullets. After running the length of three football fields, they reached the ravine and were hidden in the fog.

"Get out of here, keep under cover, and spread out," yelled James Turner and Gilbert Palmer, who were firing their rifles and covering the men's retreat.

Charlie went to the right with his gray blankets over his shoulders. That was the last time he saw his weather team.

He ran until he was so overwhelmed with exhaustion he was forced to rest. He was lying flat against the ground when he heard footsteps in the distance. He pressed his ear to the ground and listened hard. He could hear the stomping beat of the Japanese soldiers' boots closing in on him. After a moment, relief washed over him when he realized it was just the pounding of his heart. His mind then kicked into overdrive as he determined his next move.

Unarmed and alone in the fog and darkness, Charlie reasoned the Japanese would leave after they destroyed the weather station. That wouldn't take them long. Charlie's goal was to avoid capture by the Japanese. With the sun beginning to rise, he found some gray rocks and covered himself with the two gray blankets, camouflaging himself from the enemy.

Then he waited, and waited, not moving an inch. He could hear the engines of planes flying overhead and guns firing, and it was one of the longest and loneliest days in his twenty-nine years. Charlie felt as if his whole world had just been ripped out from under him.

During the month of June in Alaska, the days are long, with sixteen and a half hours of sunlight, but the fog in the Aleutians is almost always present. When night finally came, Charlie decided to make his move. His mission was to get to the tents where he and the weather team had stored their food, weapons, and ammunition. The tents were located in a ravine about two miles away.

As Charlie hurried over the rough terrain, he became overheated. When he came upon a creek, he stopped and greedily drank the cold water, and when he passed a snow drift, he packed the icy snow into his mouth. This caused him to become nauseated, and he threw up his last meal.

By the time he'd searched the area several times, the sun was beginning to rise in the east, and he still couldn't find the food and ammunition. Charlie decided to cross a stream, but he lost his balance and fell into the icy water. He was soaked and freezing cold. He was now at risk for developing acute hypothermia, and if he went into shock, he would die.

Fortunately, it turned out to be an unusually sunny day on Kiska, and Charlie laid his wet clothes out on the grass to dry. About the same time, a Japanese patrol boat pulled in and dropped anchor offshore. Charlie was in plain sight and didn't dare move.

He camouflaged himself again by covering up in the gray blankets and lying low in a creek ravine. That night he moved to a small meadow that had a view of Kiska Harbor. Although this position allowed him to keep an eye on the Japanese and would let him see when they left, it also made him visible. So he slept during the day on gray rocks covered by his gray blankets and only moved when it was dark. This strategy kept him well hidden from the Japanese.

After two days of not eating, Charlie couldn't stop thinking about food. He knew he wouldn't be able to find the food stashed in the tents, but he remembered one piece of advice from a fur trapper he'd met in Dutch Harbor. "There's nothing poisonous growing in the Aleutian Islands," the fur trapper had mistakenly told him.

Trusting that the fur trapper was right, Charlie picked what the Aleuts called *pootchki*, or wild celery, not knowing its leaves were poisonous. The tiny hairs on the stem are oily, causing rashes and blisters to break out on the skin and lips, which can last for weeks. When Charlie took his first bite into the stem, he didn't like the taste. It was bitter. So he tried peeling away the outer skin and discovered the inner flesh of the *pootchki* tasted like fresh corn on the cob. Luckily, he never ate the poisonous leaves.

A few days later, hidden by the shadows of the night, Charlie moved away from the small meadow where he had been hiding. His decision to move was easy after he had nearly been hit by bursting bullet

A Japanese tank crew on Kiska

shells from the antiaircraft guns. The American airplane pilots had been busy bombing Kiska two to three times a day, trying to force the Japanese to leave.

But the Japanese had no intention of leaving Kiska. While the U.S. government was trying to keep the Japanese invasion of Kiska and Attu a secret from the American public, the Japanese Imperial Headquarters was trying to keep their defeat at Midway a secret from the Japanese public. To boost the public's morale, they spread the news about their capture of Kiska and Attu. The news also spread to the American public through Radio Tokyo broadcasts, which were reprinted in the American newspapers and magazines.

The Japanese radio broadcasts announced that Attu and Kiska were now part of the Japanese empire and had been renamed. Attu was now called Atsuta Island, after the Atsuta shrine at Nagoya, Japan. Kiska was now known as Narukam, derived from *Narukamizunei*, one of the Japanese names for June.

The Japanese media also reported that the soldiers and their equipment had been meticulously selected, and they had brought large quantities of seeds and potatoes with them to plant gardens.

However, after forty-eight days on Kiska, the Japanese were suffering from loneliness.

"The loneliness in this remote northern base is hard to imagine," a Japanese correspondent reported. "We have received no letters or comfort bags yet.... Eating is our only pleasure. In September we will have the bitter cold Arctic winds and in the winter snow and sleet. The soldiers are all in high spirits as I watch them busily at their work, but I imagine they, too, are lonely, for loneliness is loneliness and hardships are hardships to anyone."

Like the Japanese soldiers, Charlie was suffering from loneliness and hardships, but he was also dying slowly from hunger despite spending his days eating *pootchki* and earthworms. He also spent a lot of his time trying to stay warm to ward off hypothermia, and he discovered that the dry grass was good insulation. He layered two feet of grass on the ground, then folded his blankets over it and covered them with eighteen more inches of grass. He would crawl in between the blankets, and the haystack of grass would keep him warm and dry, even if it rained directly on it.

Charlie spent his days thinking. He worried about his wife, Marie, and their baby daughter, Barbara, wondering if he would ever see them again. He dreamed about eating cheeseburgers, french fries, and apple pie and wondered how he was going to get out of this situation alive.

Since the beginning, he'd counted on the Americans invading Kiska and driving out the Japanese, but that now seemed unlikely to happen anytime soon, and Charlie was literally running out of time.

The human body can starve to death in eight weeks, and in the final stages of starvation, a person can suffer from hallucinations, convulsions, muscle pain, and heart palpitations. After seven weeks on a diet of plants and worms, Charlie only weighed eighty pounds, having lost a hundred. If he continued to evade the Japanese, he would most certainly die, but if he surrendered to the Japanese, there was a good chance they would execute him.

There was only one possibility of survival. The next morning, on July 26, 1942, Charlie started to climb the steep hill, but he was too weak and kept falling down and fainting. He thought he might die, but by sheer will he reached the summit by midmorning.

Patchy fog swirled through the tall grass and kept Charlie hidden from the Japanese soldiers who were standing by and pointing their antiaircraft guns toward the sky. After writing his name on his jacket, Charlie ripped a piece of his white undershorts. Feeling shame and humiliation, he marched toward the Japanese soldiers, waving the piece of undershorts as a surrender flag. Charlie feared for his life.

CHAPTER 4
Escape and Burn

JUNE 12, 1942. ATKA, ALASKA, FIVE DAYS AFTER THE
JAPANESE INVADED KISKA AND ATTU.

The night sky lit up like a beacon, glowing red and billowing smoke, as seventeen-year-old Larry Dirks guided his motorized skiff swiftly through the choppy water toward the raging fire that was destroying his village. He noticed that the brightest flames were ravaging the schoolhouse and the beloved onion-topped Russian Orthodox church, which contained priceless religious icons and historical records.

When he reached the beach on Nazan Bay, he quickly got out of his small boat and ran into his village. Feeling the searing heat from the fire, Larry knew he was risking his life but ignored the danger as the smoke burned his eyes and made it hard to breathe.

He needed to work fast and grab all of the food

Inside the Russian Orthodox church

and supplies he could carry. All he had were the clothes on his back and the provisions at his fishing camp, where he and the others went to take cover from the Japanese planes.

But he was too late. The general store and his home had already burned to the ground. He quickly scanned the village but discovered it was a ghost town. Reeling from the shock, Larry knew there was no one and nothing he could save, and he did the only thing he could. He got back in his skiff and left, trying to navigate through the darkness, hoping he was heading in a direction where an American ship would see him and rescue him.

Even so, the burning of Atka wouldn't be the last

shocking discovery for Larry. Soon he would learn it wasn't the invading Japanese who set his village on fire — it was the American navy.

One of the first hints that trouble was brewing in the Aleutians occurred in the summer of 1935 when a ship belonging to the Japanese Bureau of Fisheries dropped anchor in Atka's bay. A group of Japanese fishermen came ashore. They were extremely pleasant and nice to the people in Atka, even bringing them gifts and candy, but they didn't fool the Aleuts.

As friendly as the Japanese fishermen were, the Aleuts suspected these visitors were really spies, and they were right. The Japanese fishermen were, in fact, naval officers in disguise. They were busy mapping the Aleutian Islands, looking for good harbors, placing flags along the coast to help guide their ships, and determining which plants were edible.

Chief Hodikoff told U.S. government officials that the Japanese were sounding, or measuring the depth of water, and appeared to be mapping the Aleutian Chain. After a Japanese warship dropped anchor in Chichagof Harbor in Attu in 1938, he said, "We live in fear. They come all the time in their fishing boats — right up to the shore — and look and look and take our fish besides."

Although Chief Hodikoff was highly respected, the U.S. government officials seemed reluctant to listen to him or anyone else on the matter.

Even the tough-as-nails Major General Simon Bolivar Buckner, Jr., known for his roaring voice, couldn't get the U.S. government to acknowledge the potential threat that Japan was posing to Alaska. On June 5, 1942, two days before the Japanese invaded Kiska, Major General Buckner warned his superiors in Washington that Kiska was defenseless against an invasion.

Major General Simon Buckner, Jr.

The son of a Confederate general, the imposing and sharp-tongued General Buckner had a reputation for bulldozing anyone who got in his way. "I don't believe in passive warfare," he declared. "There are two ways of dealing with a rattlesnake. One is to sit still and wait for the snake to strike. The other way is to bash in the snake's head and put it out of commission. That's what I favor."

In July 1940, the U.S. Army sent General Buckner to Alaska as the head of the Alaskan Defense Command. At the time, Alaska was considered the Achilles' heel of the U.S. northern defenses.

"Even after Pearl Harbor, our so publicized naval stronghold of Dutch Harbor did not have one protecting airfield within eight hundred miles," General Buckner said. "The Jap[anese] knew this. Naturally I was concerned because my business is the defense of Dutch Harbor and Alaska."

General Buckner was in charge of securing every harbor in Alaska, building airfields and roads, and constructing his headquarters at Fort Richardson and Elmendorf Field near Anchorage. However, he had trouble getting the work started because Congress didn't want to fund these projects; instead, the defense money was being spent on what they considered more urgent concerns.

It wasn't until the fall of 1940 that construction began in full force. Congress finally gave him the much-needed money, but only approved the funds because they incorrectly believed the rumors that

Russia had built an air and submarine base on Big Diomede Island, about twenty-five miles from Alaska's mainland. At the time, Congress feared that the Russians and Germans, but not the Japanese, were going to team up and invade Alaska.

General Buckner knew this rumor wasn't true because Alaska's territorial governor, Ernest Gruening, flew over the supposed Russian base and saw that it was just a scientific research station. For once, General Buckner kept his mouth shut to get what he wanted. "We can hold Alaska or we can lose Alaska," he said. "It all depends on who gets there first."

General Buckner worked as fast as he could, but it wasn't fast enough. It was too late to protect Kiska and Attu from the invading Japanese, and concern would soon start growing that it was too late for Atka.

On June 4, 1942, the second day that Japanese planes flew over Atka on their way to drop bombs on Dutch Harbor, another plane was spotted in the sky. Everyone in Atka watched as a seaplane splashed into Nazan Bay, making an emergency landing.

Seeing that it was an American plane, the men and boys of Atka drove their motorized skiffs out

Japanese attack on Dutch Harbor

to help the pilot and crew who had been on patrol scouting the area for the enemy. The Americans were trying to get back to Dutch Harbor, but the plane, called a PBY, was almost out of fuel. Luckily, they remembered there was an emergency supply of airplane fuel stashed at Atka.

The fuel was stored in 55-gallon drums that floated in the bay, and the crew hand pumped the gas into the plane's tanks, which were located in the wings. The plane held a thousand gallons of fuel — fifty times more than the average car today — and it would take six hours to refuel it.

While the plane was being refueled, the pilot

73

went ashore and stopped in at the schoolhouse. There he met with the schoolteacher, Ruby Magee, and her husband, Ralph, and told them about the attack on Dutch Harbor.

Ruby and Ralph Magee had arrived on the island almost two years before, along with the groceries and mail, after enduring a tempestuous 365-mile, four-day journey from Unalaska onboard the *Point Reyes*, a freighter that only came to Atka twice a year. Windblown and wet, Ruby and Ralph made their way to the village that was nestled against rolling hills, stretching all the way to the rugged mountains and volatile volcanoes.

Luckily the food supply, which was also soaked from the trip, was salvageable. Otherwise, there wouldn't have been enough to eat. Although the people of Atka fished and hunted the reindeer that roamed the island and always shared what they caught with everyone in the village, they relied on the canned food that was shipped in to get through the lean and harsh winter months.

During the school year, Ruby's main job was teaching the children of Atka. Ralph was in charge of the post office, which was conveniently attached to the schoolhouse. "This did not require much work," he said, "except when the people sent out their fox pelts by insured mail once a year. We had no regular mail service. . . . Mail was brought by any vessel that happened to go out that way. One year we received our Christmas mail in May!"

Additionally, they both administered first aid to anyone who needed medical attention. Ralph talked on the radio daily to the doctor in Unalaska, reported any medical problems, and was instructed how to treat them.

However, Ralph's most important job was sending the weather reports to the naval station at Dutch Harbor every six hours. This schedule abruptly changed after the Japanese bombed it. "From that time on, I was instructed to give weather reports every hour for twelve to eighteen hours a stretch," Ralph said.

The weather was an unpredictable enemy, and the thick fog made it impossible for the U.S. military to determine which islands the Japanese had invaded.

They suspected that the Japanese might be on Kiska and Attu because Charlie House and Foster Jones had not reported the weather for days. However, it wasn't until June 10, 1942, a week after the Japanese attacked, that a break in the fog allowed both navy and air force pilots to see the Japanese firmly entrenched on Kiska and Attu.

It was also on June 10 that a naval spokesman denied the Japanese had invaded the Aleutians with the statement, "None of our inhabited islands or rocks are troubled with uninvited visitors at this time."

Although the U.S. government tried to downplay the Japanese capture of Attu and Kiska, President Franklin Delano Roosevelt gave the order to force the Japanese out of Alaska. An air raid, or blitz, was quickly put into action. The plan was to bomb Kiska and Attu continuously until the Japanese left, but this would prove to be no easy feat.

Kiska after U.S. bombing raid

Even though the U.S. military now knew where the Japanese were located, the wind, rain, and fog were deadly obstacles because they made flying planes extremely dangerous, if not impossible. The pilots said flying in the Aleutian fog was like flying in pea soup. The lack of visibility was extremely dangerous. At the time, the cockpit instruments and radar weren't advanced enough to navigate through the harsh weather conditions.

"We had some of the very first airborne radar. It was pretty primitive, with a little green scope that showed targets as pips at various points on a line across it," said Lieutenant William "Bill" Thies, a PBY pilot who was known to "fly the pants off anyone else in the squadron."

The radar used so much power from the plane's generator that the crew couldn't operate the radio and the radar at the same time. When planes came in to land, the pilots couldn't use the radar because they were required to radio in and identify themselves, so they wouldn't be mistaken for enemy planes and get shot at with antiaircraft fire.

Flying into clouds or fog, or even at night, was tricky because it was easy for a pilot to become disoriented, thinking the ground was beneath him when the plane was actually on its side, causing him to crash.

The pilots joked, "The fog is so thick you have to stick your hand out of the window to find out where you are. If your hand touches the mast of a ship, you know you're flying too low."

The cold Arctic air also posed a serious threat. The icy temperatures could cause the oil to transform into a thick jelly, preventing the plane's engine from starting. And, while in flight, the cold air combined with the fog, rain, or snow could cause ice to form on the wings, causing the plane to crash because the weight of the ice changed the plane's aerodynamics.

Compounding the problem was the fact that the U.S. military didn't have enough bomber planes, experienced pilots, or airstrips within close range of Kiska and Attu, which limited the number of attacks and weakened the prospect of forcing the Japanese out of Alaska. And, at this point in time, none of the U.S. fighter planes were a match for the almighty Japanese Zeros. The U.S. War Department's training film on plane identification warned pilots that if they spotted a Zero, they were to avoid getting into a dogfight with it if they wanted to live.

Nevertheless, the ambitious and hot-tempered

navy commander of Patrol Wing Four, Captain Leslie E. Gehres, came up with a bold plan that some would consider crazy. It required special permission from Admiral Theobald, but no one knew where Admiral Theobald was because he was still maintaining radio silence, hundreds of miles away from the action in the Aleutians.

So Captain Gehres leapfrogged Admiral Theobald's authority and went straight to Admiral Nimitz. He told him his plan, and Admiral Nimitz gave him the go-ahead.

On June 11, Captain Gehres ordered his men, who had just arrived in the Aleutians a few days prior

PBY plane

from sunny San Diego, to dive-bomb the Japanese around the clock, *regardless of the weather*. They were not to stop until they either ran out of bombs or the Japanese left Alaska.

The idea was crazy because the PBY scouting planes Captain Gehres's pilots flew were not designed to dive-bomb, and some didn't have radar, so flying in the fog was suicidal.

Slow moving and ducklike in appearance, this lightly armored plane was an easy target. There was typically a crew of seven onboard: a pilot, copilot, navigator, crew chief, radioman, and two gunners. The PBY was designed for antisubmarine warfare and was loaded with two 500-pound bombs, two massive .50 caliber machine guns, and one .30 caliber stinger machine gun that extended below the plane's tail, which was to be used if a Japanese plane snuck up from behind.

Despite being lightly armed with weapons, the hulking PBYs' main job was to scout the area for enemy planes, submarines, and ships, and then report their findings to the fighter pilots who would take over. They also searched for planes that were shot down and rescued the crews, using their pontoons to land on water. PBY pilots had never been in a situation where it was necessary to dive-bomb, a skill that required intensive training — but now there was no time for that.

There was a small window of opportunity to blast the Japanese out of the Aleutians before they had enough time to fortify their position. Since Captain Gehres had twenty-four PBY "flying boats" moored at Nazan Bay in Atka, he was in a position to strike back relentlessly.

Strategically, the PBYs were in a good location. Atka, which is sandwiched almost midway between Kiska and Dutch Harbor, was three hundred miles closer to Kiska than any other airstrip. But, since the PBY is a seaplane, it didn't need an airstrip and could land right on Nazan Bay. The navy PBYs could bomb Kiska every hour, while the army's bomber pilots had to fly six hundred miles from the airstrip in Umnak, plus any added distance to navigate storms, find an opening in the fog, and locate their target. This took about ten hours, allowing them to fly only two missions a day.

This was a punishing plan for the PBY crews, and Captain Gehres knew they were on a death mission. "Every flight was a flight the crew should not have returned from," he said. "Every man knew this and yet none wavered."

Without delay, the PBYs were loaded with all available bombs and ammunition. The villagers from Atka did what they could to help. The Atkan men and boys pumped the gas and raised the bombs up into the wing racks.

"Several of the native kids who helped our PBY crew in this work . . . could not have been more than twelve years of age," said nineteen-year-old Paul Carrigan, aerographer's mate and combat aircrew member of Patrol Wing Four. "It was truly a cooperative effort . . . working desperately together for a common cause."

The Kiska Blitz began in full force on the morning of June 11, 1942. Lieutenant Commander Carroll "Doc" Jones figured out the best way to dive-bomb the unwieldy PBY. The visibility problem was solved by flying above the blanket of fog, but this also created another problem. By flying above the clouds, they were up too high to drop a bomb. So the pilots searched for an elusive hole in the cloud ceiling. Once the hole was found, the crew hoped for the best as the pilot pushed the nose of the plane down into the death plunge.

As the speed of the plane increased to nearly 250 mph, the plane's wings shook violently. Pilots were careful not to exceed this speed because the stress of pulling out of the dive could cause the wings to rip off. As they continued to plunge, the wind howled through the openings around the gun blisters in the plane.

The first time the Japanese saw the scouting planes dive through the clouds, they couldn't believe their eyes. They had never seen anything like it. The announcer on Radio Tokyo would soon report that the Americans had a new type of dive-bomber that looked very similar to a PBY, not realizing that it was a PBY.

But the Japanese were ready for an American attack. Their antiaircraft encampments were dotted along the cliffs of Kiska Harbor. When they spotted a PBY diving through a cloud opening, the Japanese pointed their machine guns and cannons toward it and fired away. The machine-gun bullets could easily rip through the PBY's thin armor plate. This forced the PBY pilots to quickly change their strategy. They started to avoid the breaks in clouds and dive directly through the thick bank of fog.

The PBYs targeted the heavy cruisers, light cruisers, destroyers, and transporters in Kiska Harbor. The PBYs kept plunging until they were terrifyingly close to the water. As the bombs dropped from the wing racks, the pilots had to work quickly to get out of the way. They didn't want to get blasted by their own bombs. This was the hardest and most death defying part of dive-bombing — getting back up into the cover of the fog.

Both pilots were needed to yank the steering wheel back, and the effort forced the pilots to nearly stand up.

Ensign Bill King, who was one of the first to dive-bomb a PBY, said, "You level off and zoom back into the soup as fast as you can, which is pretty fast, because the dive gives you extra speed. After that you feel to see if you're in one piece and then you call the plane captain [crew chief] and ask him to count the wounded."

Within minutes of the first PBY dive-bombing attack on Kiska, three navy crewmen were dead. Some of the PBYs did not make it back to Nazan Bay, and those that did were riddled with hundreds of bullet holes. One plane was filled with so many holes it sank when it landed.

"They were shot up," said Larry Dirks. "Some men on these planes were dead and some wounded. Having seen this, our people were getting more scared. Even I was getting more scared."

Nevertheless, everyone did what they could to help. Ruby Magee donated the school's supply of pencils, which were broken in half and jammed into the PBYs' bullet holes.

The crew of the USS *Gillis*, a seaplane tender anchored in Nazan Bay, worked nonstop. Only twice the size of a PBY, and skippered by the gregarious Lieutenant Commander Norman L. Garton, the *Gillis* didn't have enough room to accommodate the extra 238 men flying the PBYs in the Kiska Blitz, but they made do.

Without complaints, the crew on the *Gillis* cooked meals around the clock and gave up their bunk beds to the PBY men so they could sleep for a precious two to three hours before heading off on another bombing mission. One PBY crew was sent on three fifteen-hour bombing missions with only three hours of rest in between them.

The spillover from the PBY crews was taken to the village of Atka. Ruby gave them blankets, hot coffee, and fresh water to wash with.

"The crews from these planes came over to the schoolhouse to sleep on the floor in the schoolroom and in our [separate] quarters," Ralph Magee said. "We turned our place over to them to use as they could."

On the morning of June 12, just one day after the start of the Kiska Blitz, the navy ordered the Aleuts to move to their fishing camp, which was three miles away. It was felt they would be safer there, out of harm's way.

"They were evacuated while eating breakfast," a navy officer reported. "And the eggs were still on the table — coffee in the cups. A lot of their personal clothing and stuff was still hanging in closets."

With the exception of Ruby and Ralph Magee, no one other than medical personnel was allowed in the village of Atka. But soon after the residents were sent to their fishing camp a full-blown emergency erupted.

Flying in low, a Japanese scouting plane circled the village and opened fire with its machine guns. No one was hurt and nothing was damaged, but Admiral Nimitz knew from intercepted messages and code cracking that "the Japanese commander in Kiska had directed his aircraft to bomb Nazan Bay."

The fear of the Japanese bombing Atka and starting a blitz prompted a snap decision. This decision would not only create chaos but it would turn deadly.

At eight P.M. Commander Garton received his orders: "Destroy the Atka village and evacuate all the citizens."

"We could have twenty minutes to prepare to

leave the village," said Ralph Magee. "He [Lieutenant Commander Garton] had orders to burn all the buildings before the Japanese could come and take over. . . . We were told to get the people aboard the tender and we'd all be taken to Dutch Harbor. There wasn't time to get word to the fish[ing] camp, so he told the two of us to get aboard. The village was then set afire by the navy men."

At 2:24 A.M., on June 13, the *Gillis* left Nazan Bay, carrying Ruby and Ralph Magee as well as the bodies of the men who had been killed in the Kiska Blitz.

The outcome of the blitz was bleak. The damage from the bombing was "never accurately determined," according to the official record from Patrol Wing Four, with the exception of damaging the Japanese destroyer *Hibiki*. The *Chicago Daily Times* reported that the bombs destroyed three Japanese cruisers and a large Japanese transport. Yet, despite the sixty-five thousand tons of bombs reportedly dropped, the Japanese weren't leaving and the Americans were retreating.

When daybreak came, the USS *Hulbert*, another seaplane tender, found Larry Dirks in his skiff, heading away from Atka and brought him onboard.

The *Hulbert* had orders to evacuate the people of Atka, but no one was there.

"We went into a bay, which we used to call *Sviiniya*, thinking perhaps other of our people might be there," said Larry. "The boat's captain circled the bay, and since we did not see any signs of life there, he went back out of the bay and went through a pass [strait]."

The captain then dropped anchor in Nazan Bay and tried to signal the others to come out of hiding by flashing a searchlight.

"Finally, some of the people started showing up in their skiffs," said Larry.

Braving the rough waters, families with children and babies nearly capsized in their boats as they made their way to the *Hulbert*. On June 13, at 5:22 A.M., the *Hulbert* left Nazan Bay heading for Dutch Harbor with sixty-two Aleuts, leaving twenty-one behind.

Larry felt immense sadness and grief; he was "in tears . . . knowing that we were leaving our island. We were not really sure if everyone from Atka had been taken away."

Just two hours after Larry left on the *Hulbert*, Japanese seaplanes named Kawanishi H6K, code name Mavis, flew over Atka. The Mavis seaplane has four engines and a crew of nine men, and can carry a load of bombs weighing 2,200 pounds. The Japanese bombed the village, then flew over the fishing camp and machine gunned the tents. Luckily, no one was killed because the remaining Aleuts had already left to hide on a small island in Atka Bay.

On June 15, two days after the Japanese bombed Atka, two PBYs flew into Nazan Bay and set off flares. The twenty-one remaining Aleuts cautiously came out to the seaplanes, boarded them, and were promptly evacuated.

But this wasn't the end of the evacuations from the Aleutian Islands. It was only the beginning.

The USS *Delarof* hurriedly evacuated the 477 Aleuts in the Pribilof Islands. Two days later, on

USS *Delarof*

June 17, they picked up the 83 Atka Aleuts in Dutch Harbor. The ship, which had a passenger capacity of 376, now had 560 Aleuts onboard.

When the Aleuts left Dutch Harbor, they had no idea where they were being taken. When they asked where they were going, no one could tell them because no one actually knew their final destination, not even the captain. The evacuation happened so quickly, there was no plan. But one thing was certain. Their nightmare was just beginning, and many would not survive.

Aleuts being evacuated

CHAPTER 5
Dead Man Walking

JULY 26, 1942. KISKA, ALASKA, THE DAY CHARLIE HOUSE
SURRENDERED TO THE JAPANESE.

When Charlie walked toward the Japanese soldiers, they saw a ghost in the fog. His eyes protruded from his skull and his cheeks were hollowed out. His clothes hung loosely from his skeletal body.

Charlie could barely stand after the long walk. The Japanese soldiers rushed toward him, held him up by his elbows, and then immediately sat him down and fed him biscuits and tea.

As Charlie ate, a group of American B-17 bombers flew overhead, and the Japanese began shooting at them. After dropping their bombs, the planes flew away, and the Japanese officer in charge came over to Charlie.

He was angry and yelled orders at some of the soldiers. Charlie didn't understand what was being said, but he had serious misgivings when they adjusted their bayonets in their sheaths and the officer motioned for Charlie to follow him down a path.

The thought of getting slaughtered by the bayonets weighed heavily on Charlie's mind, but he somehow summoned the courage to follow. After a short walk, Charlie saw where he was being led and was shocked.

He was right back where he started forty-nine days ago. Not only could he see the three shacks where his weather team had lived, but there were now another twenty-four structures that the Japanese had built.

Photo of Charlie House and his wife, Marie, that he carried in his pocket while a POW

Despite the ankle-deep mud and continuous bombing by the Americans, the Japanese had managed to install telegraph and power poles, fire hydrants, and a defensive fortification. They had also built roads, three power plants, and a water storage tank. Plus, the camp headquarters not only had a seaplane and submarine base, three radio stations, and a telephone system, but also a newly dug network of hillside tunnels. These tunnels protected them from the daily American bombardment, and also housed the hospital and sleeping quarters. Outside, the Japanese had planted gardens and built six Shinto shrines.

A glimmer of hope lifted Charlie's spirits. "I had the feeling of being spared again," he said.

They sat Charlie down on a grass sack, and a circle of Japanese soldiers stood around him and just stared. They were surprised and in utter disbelief — but mostly impressed — that he had managed to survive the unforgiving Aleutian wilderness. They had been certain he had succumbed to death weeks ago.

The soldiers immediately gave him some dinner, tea, and more biscuits. While he ate, the Japanese soldiers continued to stare, and stare. They stared at him for several hours.

"I had the feeling of a monkey in a zoo," Charlie said.

In the evening, they gave Charlie a grass sack and some blankets. They had him sleep in the powerhouse shack, the same place where he and Walter were shot out of bed. As Charlie lay down to rest, he could see the Japanese soldiers peeping through the window. A long line formed as each soldier stared at Charlie for a minute, then gave the next soldier in line a turn to take a look at him. It wasn't until darkness fell and it became hard to see that they stopped staring.

Charlie could hear the rain tapping on the asphalt roof. It had rained every day but one since the Japanese invaded.

"It sure felt cozy to have shelter again," Charlie said.

That night, a Japanese guard shined a flashlight into Charlie's eyes every half hour to make sure he was still alive. The next morning, Captain Kanzaki brought war correspondent Mikizo Fukazawa to see Charlie so he could write a story for the Japanese newspaper *Domei*. That's when Charlie found out the fate of his nine-man weather team.

When they entered the room, Charlie kicked

away his blankets and sat up. Mikizo noticed right away that Charlie had "the friendliest of smiles" although his salute, which he was now required to do to show his respect to the Japanese officers, was a little shaky.

"His eyes were unnaturally large in contrast to his sunken cheeks," Mikizo said. "And his emaciated limbs were so thin they were like sticks."

"When our detachment launched the surprise attack on Kiska Island, there were ten American soldiers stationed on the island," Captain Kanzaki said. "We managed to capture nine of them, but we couldn't track down the tenth. Finally, we decided that he had probably perished from the cold or from hunger somewhere in the mists and called off the search. . . . This was the man we sought."

In the Japanese hunt for the ten-man weather team, Rolland Coffield, the chief pharmacist (or medic) and John McCandless, the cook, were the first two captured, just a few hours after the Japanese landed on Kiska. Although Rolland and John were well hidden in the fog, so were the Japanese, and the two ran right into Japanese soldiers.

The soldiers confiscated their weapons, tied their hands, and pointed their bayonets at them. Under interrogation, John and Rolland were asked how many men were on Kiska, what kind of weapons they had, and where they were hiding. Then they were forced to cook some food from their icebox and eat it to show the Japanese it wasn't poisoned.

The next to be captured were James Turner, Lethayer Eckles, and Gilbert Palmer. They had spent the night in an abandoned Aleut *barabara*. On the second day, when they were trying to figure out how to get to their food stash and an abandoned dory, the Japanese spotted them hiding in the tall beach grass. The Japanese soldiers surrounded them, took their rifles, and searched them. James was singled out. The soldiers took him into a small office where there were about six more officers. Two of them beat and slapped him because they thought he was rude and disrespectful, but they also beat him because they thought he was withholding information, which he was. James wasn't about to tell them what the antennas were for.

"I told them all I knew was the weather and very little of that because I hadn't been there very long," James said.

The Japanese wasted no time putting the captured men on a cargo ship the next day and sending them to a prison camp in Japan. They would arrive in Yososuka ten days later, on June 19, 1942.

The remaining members of the weather team, Walter Winfrey, Robert Christensen, Madison Courtenay, and Wilford Gaffey, also surrendered to the Japanese. They lasted a week in the unforgiving Aleutian wilderness, finding shelter in abandoned *barabaras*. Each *barabara* had some food left behind by the fur trappers, and they also foraged for mussels from the rocks and collected driftwood near the shore. Their dog, Explosion, also inadvertently helped out by cornering a blue fox and tussling with it until Wilfred stepped in with a club.

"That night we had fox stew," Walter said.

On June 13, 1942, the last day of the Kiska Blitz, and two days before they surrendered, the four men watched as a PBY flew in and dropped a bomb on Vega Bay, about a thousand yards from where they took cover in a shallow ravine.

Explosion was at his wit's end with all of the noise from the machine guns and bombs. He had a habit of running around willy-nilly and barking like crazy at the sound of gunfire, but if they wanted to stay safe, they needed to be quiet and still. So Walter lay on top of Explosion and muzzled him.

When the bombing and machine-gun fire stopped, they made their way back to a *barabara* in Gertrude Cove. They stayed there for two days but they were running out of food.

"By that time the fox stew was at an end," Walter said. "It tasted pretty bad even though we were starving."

Their hunger pangs prompted them to backtrack from their current camp to look for the food cache in a *barabara* on Sand Beach. They knew that the fur trapper had left behind a supply of food that would last six months if they rationed it carefully.

They hiked over the mountains for five hours. With each step Walter took, he was reminded of the bullet lodged in his leg, but he ignored the pain. He had no choice if he wanted to survive.

When they arrived, it was a "bitter disappointment," Walter said. The Japanese soldiers had destroyed the *barabara* and taken all the food.

They started hiking back to their camp at Gertrude Cove, making it halfway up the mountain before it started to sleet. They were wet, cold, hungry, and exhausted from walking against the powerful Aleutian wind.

"We could have never made it," Walter said. "So

the only other alternative was to turn [ourselves] in to the Jap[anese] and take our chances or starve in the hills."

They threw down their rifles and ammunition, and at 5:30 P.M. on June 15, 1942, eight days after the Japanese invaded Kiska, Walter, Robert, Madison, and Wilford found some Japanese soldiers working on the beach and surrendered.

"Guards came running from all over," Walter said.

They were taken to their former cookhouse, and one of the first questions they were asked was where was Charlie House.

"We told them we believed he was dead," Walter said.

The men were fed rice and soup that night, and the next day they were interrogated. They were asked if the bay was mined, if there were any more food stashes, and where was Charlie House. Again, Walter told them he thought Charlie was dead.

When Walter told them about the bullet that was still in his leg, the Japanese officer seemed "greatly concerned" and called in the doctor.

The doctor gave Walter a shot of Novocain, removed the bullet, carefully stitched the wound, and bandaged it.

The following night, they were put on an old coal-burning transport ship heading back to Japan. When they arrived, about June 27, they were blindfolded and taken to a navy base and kept there until Walter's bullet wound healed. On July 2, 1942, the men were transferred to Ofuna interrogation camp, one of the worst prison camps in Japan.

After Charlie heard the news that his team was captured but still alive, a Japanese doctor bustled through the door.

"He's had hardly anything to eat for over fifty days, except for the grass growing on the shore," Captain Kanzaki told the doctor. "When we gave him some rice gruel, he gulped down so much he got sick."

As if on cue, Charlie pressed down on his stomach with his hands.

"He was so thin that from the side he resembled a wooden plank," Mikizo Fukazawa, the news correspondent, said. "The thighs were no thicker than the arms of a child."

The doctor asked Charlie if he knew that Pearl Harbor had been attacked by the Japanese.

"I know," Charlie said.

"You know the American aircraft carrier *Saratoga* was sunk in the Battle of Coral Sea?" the doctor asked, trying to mislead Charlie with misinformation.

"No, I didn't know that."

"The Japanese army has already taken the Aleutian Islands," the doctor said. "You still think the Americans can win the war?"

Charlie remained silent.

The doctor changed his line of questioning and asked Charlie about his background in the navy and his family. Charlie's friendly expression turned serious.

"When you return to Tokyo," said Charlie to Mikizo Fukazawa, "please send my wife and daughter a telegram saying that I'm safe and under the protection of the Japanese army, so they won't worry."

Charlie carefully spelled out the names and address of his wife and daughter in California.

The Japanese newspaper reporter was incredulous. He couldn't believe Charlie's request.

"I felt sorry for him," Fukazawa said. "But deep in my heart I was thinking about something else. What if he had been a Japanese soldier? It would be unthinkable for a healthy Japanese soldier to allow himself to be taken prisoner. Even if he had been injured and consequently captured, not only would no Japanese act so friendly toward his captors, it would not even occur to him to plead for a message to be delivered to his family stating that he was alive and well. As I listened to this man, I learned a lesson in the differences between Japanese and Americans."

The telegram was never sent.

For the next three weeks, the Japanese gave Charlie all the food he could eat, so he would gain weight. Once he regained his strength, they put him to work. He spent his days with other Japanese workers, filling sandbags.

But that came to an end on September 20, 1942. Two months after Charlie surrendered, he was put on a cargo ship departing for Japan. When he was told to go into the hatch where they kept the coal, he was greeted by Chief Mike Hodikoff and the Attuans, who were also onboard.

Their fate would remain a mystery until after the war.

CHAPTER 6
Fighters, Bombers, and Cutthroats

SEPTEMBER 14, 1942. KISKA, ALASKA.

Six days before Charlie was loaded onto a cargo ship heading for Japan, he heard a loud droning noise while he was filling sandbags with the other Japanese workers on the beach in Kiska. Looking up into the sky, he saw fourteen P-39 Airacobra fighter planes dive down and continue flying dangerously low over the harbor. The Americans were on their way to drop more bombs on Kiska.

The P-39 Airacobra fighter planes came in first, attacking the Japanese antiaircraft defenses while the P-38 Lightning fighter planes attacked the Japanese Zero fighter seaplanes (Allied codename Rufes), which were sitting ducks, bobbing up and down in the water.

Behind these fighters were twelve B-24 Liberators and one B-17 Flying Fortress. Once the fighter planes weakened the Japanese's defenses, the bombers headed toward the main camp with their machine guns firing.

The American pilots planned on taking the Japanese by surprise, flying in low so the Japanese radar couldn't detect them. Unfortunately, the day was so clear that the Japanese could see them coming.

The fourteen P-38 Lightnings opened fire on the camp with their machine guns. Bullets were flying everywhere. Twelve B-24 Liberators followed closely, flying as low as fifty feet, unloading their bombs on the area below.

Kiska bombing

A Japanese officer had told Charlie he was supposed to always go into the powerhouse for shelter. Instead, he ran for cover into a narrow underground tunnel. He was too tall to stand up, but he didn't care.

"I was reluctant to run through that mess of gunfire and dropping bombs," Charlie said.

The bombs shook the earth, kicking up the claylike mud. Ten buildings caught on fire and burned black smoke. One bomb fell through the roof of the weather team's powerhouse. It landed squarely on Charlie's blankets and blew out a wall.

Belatedly, the Japanese pilots fired up the five Rufes that weren't destroyed in the attack and took to the air, dogfighting with the Airacobras. Two P-38 Lightnings went after the same Rufe and collided. The American fighters burst into flames on impact, killing everyone onboard. In the end, the fourteen Airacobras outnumbered the Rufes, and every Japanese plane went down in flames.

By the time the air raid was over, two Japanese ships had been sunk, three ships were on fire, three midget submarines were destroyed, and four hundred Japanese were dead or wounded.

This was the first major air attack from the new

top secret air base in the Andreandof Islands in the Aleutians —Adak to be precise, just 240 miles away. Now a round-trip flight, including time to find the target and drop bombs, was less than three hours.

The intensity of the war increased as the bombing raids on Kiska became more frequent and effective. On October 14, four weeks later, the heaviest coordinated raid was made on Kiska. On the mission were six B-26 Marauders, nine B-24 Liberators, twelve P-38 Lightnings, and one B-17 Flying Fortress. As the P-38 Lightnings protected the B-24s from antiaircraft fire, the B-24s flew in low and dropped fire bombs on the main Japanese camp and 500-pound bombs on the submarine base.

Ten minutes later, the B-26 Marauders flew one hundred feet off the water into Gertrude Cove and dropped torpedoes, trying to hit a freighter but missing. One torpedo ran up onto the beach and exploded, while another one got stuck in the mud at the bottom of the cove.

After the last American bomber and fighter planes headed home, a lone B-17 bomber stayed behind, circling Kiska. Looking out over the left wing of the plane, the six-man crew — the pilot, copilot, bombardier-navigator, top turret gunner, tail gunner, and a radioman — could see the orange flames and black billowing smoke in the burning camp.

Sitting in the pilot's seat, clad in a leather jacket with his wife's silk stocking wrapped discreetly around his neck for good luck, was the mustached Colonel William O. Eareckson, Eric to his bomber friends, Wild Bill to his navy friends, and Colonel E to the lower-ranking men. He was the head of the Eleventh Air Force Bomber Command and the mastermind behind the low-level attacks on Kiska.

Since the fog in the Aleutians made it difficult to locate targets and drop bombs from the usual five thousand feet, Eric figured out a way to solve this problem. He trained his pilots to fly in low over the water at thirty to forty feet. This broke the cardinal rule of aviation that a pilot should always maintain a high altitude to avoid crashing into ground obstacles and provide a safety net in case the plane has technical problems.

At such a low level, the pilot, who was also in charge of pushing the button to drop the bomb, had to gauge it just right so the bomb would skip across the water like a stone, hitting ships and seaplanes. Eric also developed a four-and-a-half second delay

Colonel Eric Eareckson instructing his bomber pilots

fuse for the bombs so the pilot had enough time to pull up and get away before it blew up.

However, flying in low made the planes easy targets for antiaircraft fire. So the fighter planes, which were equipped with .50 caliber machine guns that could rip through the armor plates of a destroyer, went in first and obliterated the antiaircraft fire coming from the destroyers and the weapons on land. This helped protect the heavy bombers from being shot down as they flew in afterward and dropped their big bombs.

In the air, there was no denying that Eric was the top dog, more than capable of flying all types of planes and working in any position on the crew. He went on nearly every mission because, as always, he never asked anyone to do something that he wouldn't do himself.

"I wanted to show the kids it was all right; that if I could do it, they could," said Eric.

He also liked to photograph the damage and, if the opportunity presented itself — which it always did when Eric was in the pilot's seat — unload some bombs.

After snapping several photos, Eric circled around, looking for his target, the Japanese shore installations, while weaving in and out of the clouds to avoid the antiaircraft guns, all of which were pointed directly at him. A large hole in the clouds gave him the opportunity he needed to dive-bomb the target.

Peering through the bombsight control, he dropped through the hole and ignored the *ack-ack-ack* of machine guns firing away. A bullet tore into the left wing, and the plane suddenly jerked upward. Eric expertly righted the plane.

But more bullets ripped through the plane, tearing a hole in the gas tank. In the hailstorm of bullets, Eric suddenly lifted himself out of his seat and reached down to pick up a bullet. It was from a Japanese machine gun.

"Why the nerve of those so-and-sos. They're shooting at me now!" said Eric, keeping his eyes focused on the target and his finger on the bomb release button. After unloading the last bomb, Eric was finally satisfied and he headed back to Adak. The first low-level bombing attack on Kiska was a success.

Colonel Eareckson writing a message to the Japanese on a bomb he's going to drop

On August 28, 1942, two and half weeks before the first air raid on Kiska from Adak, in the middle of the night, two submarines surfaced near the shore of Adak. Quickly and quietly, two dozen men climbed onto five rubber rafts and paddled against the Aleutian wind. It was four miles to the shore.

At first glance, it was obvious they weren't typical soldiers. In fact, they didn't look like soldiers at all. They didn't wear uniforms, or insignia, and some preferred to wear buckskin jackets.

Leading this pack of unusual-looking soldiers was a man with a bald head and a scar on his face. His name was Colonel Lawrence Castner, and he was in charge of what was officially called the Alaska Combat Intelligence Platoon, also known as the Alaska Scouts. Everyone called them Castner's Cutthroats.

A soldier couldn't apply to become one of Castner's Cutthroats; Castner came for you. He handpicked each one. They were a mix of hunters, fishermen, prospectors, and trappers, and some were Eskimos, American Indians, and Aleuts. What they all had in common was their ability to live off the land and survive in the Alaskan wilderness all alone, and none of them liked to follow the rules.

Their main job was to spy on the Japanese and gather intelligence without being detected or leaving a trace of their existence — a Cutthroat was so stealthy that he could crawl through tall grass while barely moving it. They also knew Morse code, surveying, and mapmaking, and their maps were crucial in helping the other troops determine where to safely land.

Castner's right-hand man was the hard-bitten Major William Verbeck. Like all Cutthroats, he carried his own weapons of choice, and his knife was one of his prized possessions. He'd asked a surgeon to design the blade so when he stabbed someone the blade would go in and out with ease.

Major Verbeck, who also spoke Japanese, trained the Cutthroats to fight like commandos — hand-to-hand combat that included silent kills from a short distance.

"Aleut Pete"

Another of Colonel Castner's most valuable cutthroats was Simeon Pletnikoff, nicknamed Aleut Pete. Colonel Castner chose Aleut Pete because he was born and raised in the Aleutians. He was a highly skilled trapper and hunter, plus he knew the land and ocean, which was vital for charting and mapmaking.

This war was very personal to him because Chief Hodikoff was his relative. His girlfriend also lived on Attu when the Japanese invaded. He didn't know if either was dead or alive.

Tonight he and the others were potential targets for the Japanese as they skulked onto Adak to find out if the Japanese occupied it. General Buckner had big plans for Adak.

Logistically and strategically, the U.S. military needed an airstrip and base that was closer to the Japanese invaders. Currently, the closest airstrip was Fort Glenn on Umnak Island, six hundred miles from Kiska. An airstrip on Adak would allow the bomber and fighter pilots to make more air raids. Aleut Pete and the other Cutthroats were to map the island, looking for a place to build an airfield. And if they found any Japanese soldiers on Adak, their orders were to kill them on the spot.

As the Cutthroats scoured the island, some hiking forty-five miles, they looked for the enemy while it rained and the icy wind blew. No Japanese soldiers were found, and they discovered that the only flat area on Adak was the lagoon. In order to build an airstrip, the lagoon would have to be drained.

The Cutthroats signaled a PBY pilot flying overhead with a green cloth, a code for "all clear." The word was out that the enemy was not on Adak. The Cutthroats' mission was accomplished, and a new air base was quickly built.

Little did they know that when the Japanese discovered this new air base, it would be a pivotal point that would lead to an all-out war.

With the new air base in Adak, Eric and the other bomber pilots were now close enough to conduct continuous air raids. The goal was to get the Japanese out of the Aleutians as soon as possible.

An all-important weather station was set up on Adak, so the pilots knew when they could fly, and four more ten-man weather teams were set up in isolated outposts across the Aleutians. However, this time, some of Castner's Cutthroats were assigned to support and protect them.

St. Paul Island

General Buckner also deployed some of his soldiers to Atka, St. Paul Island in the Pribilofs, as well as Seguam and Tanaga islands, part of the Andreanof Islands in the central Aleutians.

What the Americans didn't know at the time was that the Japanese didn't plan on staying in the Aleutians through the winter. In fact, the Japanese soldiers had left Attu and moved to Kiska, and the Japanese planned to move everyone to the Kurile Islands, fifteen hundred miles from Kiska, where the Japanese had a military base. But when a Japanese reconnaissance plane discovered the Americans had a new air base on Adak, and they learned American soldiers were in other parts of the Aleutians, the Japanese felt threatened. Now the Americans were not only closer to their troops on Kiska, but were in a position to launch an invasion of Japan. In this assumption, they were absolutely correct. From the strategically located Adak, General Buckner planned to oust the Japanese from the Aleutians and start a northern invasion of Japan.

As a result, the Japanese Imperial Headquarters abandoned their plan to leave the Aleutians in the winter. Their new plan was to occupy the Aleutians forever.

Japanese officers on Attu

On October 29, 1942, under the command of Lieutenant Colonel Hiroshi Yanekawa, Japan sent more troops to occupy Attu and to build an airfield. The U.S. military didn't even know the Japanese were back until November 7, when one of Eric's pilots flew over Attu and noticed the enemy — a week and a half after they had arrived.

For the U.S. military, their next move was to set up another air base on Amchitka Island, just forty-five miles from Kiska, in January 1943. They also planned to starve the Japanese out of Attu and Kiska with a naval blockade. The last ship to bring food and supplies to the Japanese on Attu arrived on March 10. Against the odds, the Americans successfully blockaded the Japanese supply ships.

However, trying to starve them out didn't work. The Japanese supplemented their supply of rice, sake, and tea by fishing and digging for clams.

The Japanese were steadfastly refusing to leave.

Their orders were "to hold the western Aleutians at all costs."

This left one last option for General Buckner. In order to oust the Japanese from the Aleutians, American soldiers would have to go to Attu and Kiska and fight them.

The plan, called Operation Landcrab, was to circumvent Kiska and take back Attu first. The American troops would surround the Japanese and squeeze them out. It would be an underwater assault coupled with air strikes led by Eric and his bomber pilots with reinforcements from the Royal

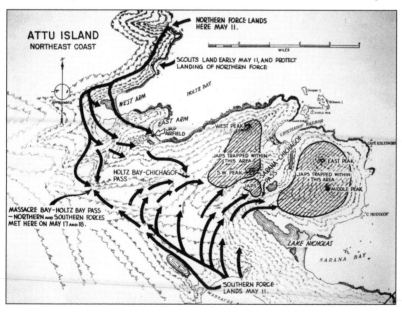

U.S. strategy map for Attu

Canadian Air Force. The War Department agreed to assign a special combat unit from California to increase the number of troops. Castner's Cutthroats were going into combat, too.

The Americans were confident that the battle would last three days — at most. What they hadn't counted on was that the Japanese knew they were coming.

By the time the Americans realized that they had severely underestimated the Japanese soldiers' strength, honor, and sheer determination, it was too late. They found themselves fighting in one of the bloodiest and deadliest hand-to-hand combat battles against Japan.

CHAPTER 7
The Last Banzai

The roar of the Caterpillar tractors could be heard throughout the night while the U.S. soldiers tried to sleep in their soggy and mud-caked sleeping bags. The noise from the engine and wheels had replaced the sounds of guns firing and grenades exploding amidst anguished cries of pain and loss. The sound of the tractors moving through the wet and spongy tundra signaled the end of the bloodbath, but it wasn't much of a relief. It was only a merciless reminder of the nightmare.

Trailers were attached to the tractors to collect the corpses that were scattered for miles in the ankle-deep mud. The drivers maneuvered the large wheels so they didn't accidentally push the dead bodies deeper into the mud.

The men who were collecting the dead bodies

sometimes seemed calm and efficient as they carried out the grim task. Other times it was just too much for them to bear, and they vomited.

Thousands of dead bodies lay haphazardly across the killing field. Some had been killed by gunshot wounds, some by bayonets, and others by exploding grenades. The lifeless bodies were mangled or blown into pieces, often beyond recognition.

For once, the notoriously bad Aleutian weather was finally working in everyone's favor. The temperature was a chilly forty degrees Fahrenheit, preserving the thousands of dead bodies. The men collecting the dead needed time for such a big job.

Some of the bodies were examined to determine the cause of death, and some of the pockets of

Wounded U.S. soldier on Attu

the dead soldiers were searched for any personal belongings, which were then placed in a clean wool sock for safekeeping. They also looked for each dead soldier's dog tags, which identified him by name. One tag was left around his neck, and the other was nailed to a grave marker. Finally, a set of fingerprints was taken. Each body was wrapped in a tan-colored blanket, ready for burial. There weren't any caskets.

It would take days to bury all of the dead. Bulldozers were also busy digging mass graves where there wouldn't be any grave markers. When every last dead soldier was finally buried, it would mark the end of a battle that shocked every person who lived through it.

It was about noon on May 11, 1943, when Aleut Pete and the other Castner's Cutthroats silently rowed plastic dories through the dense fog toward Red Beach on Attu. The invasion to take back the island had officially begun. Technically, it was already supposed to be over, but they were late getting started. For the last four days, the fog and stormy weather had made it impossible to reach Attu safely.

Since General Buckner didn't have enough combat forces of his own for the battle on Attu, the War Department assigned the Seventh Infantry Division. This specialized combat group of ten thousand men was brought in for the bloody job of blasting the Japanese soldiers out of their foxholes, trenches, and bunkers.

U.S. soldiers at Attu

The U.S. plan of attack involved dividing the Seventh Infantry into four groups: the Northern Force, the Southern Force, the Scout Battalion, and the Reserve Group, which would wait onboard a ship. The strategy was for the Northern, Southern, and Scout Battalion forces to close in on the Japanese from three different points. The idea was to push them toward Chichagof Valley (near the village of Attu) and trap them. The Northern and Southern Forces would meet midway and take on the Japanese together. The Scout Battalion was to make sure the Japanese didn't retreat into the mountains where they could hide out and prolong the battle for months. There would also be a naval bombardment and air attacks from Eric and his pilots.

The only problem — and it was a big one — was that the Seventh Infantry was completely unprepared for the cold and rainy Aleutian climate. Their specialty was desert combat, and they arrived in the Aleutians wearing short-sleeve fatigues and leather boots, which offered no protection from the rain and snow. Nevertheless, the higher-ups didn't think inadequate clothing was a concern because they believed the battle was only going to last for three days. This would be a costly and deadly miscalculation.

Another big problem was that no one had a reliable map. In fact, some areas on the map they did have were blank. This was why Aleut Pete and the other Cutthroats were sent ashore before the Seventh Division Northern Force, to check out the area. The six landing craft poised behind the Cutthroats were waiting to hear if it was even possible to land on Red Beach.

It was. The beach was narrow, making the landing tricky, but not impossible. A few hours later fifteen hundred men were onshore and, surprisingly, not a single shot was fired by the Japanese.

Earlier, in the predawn hours, Captain William Willoughby and his group of 244 men of the Scout Battalion successfully landed on Beach Scarlet in Austin Cove. Shivering in the chilly temperature, and with only enough food to last for a day and a half, they began their slog up the snowy and rugged mountains. No enemy was in sight.

The Southern Force landed on Massacre Bay (so named because in 1745 the Russian fur hunters murdered fifteen Attuans there) by mid afternoon in fog so thick that some of the boats ended up on the wrong beach. Like the Northern Force and Scout Battalion, once the troops landed on the treeless island, they immediately took cover in the rocky foothills, without a single shot being fired by the Japanese.

What the U.S. soldiers would soon discover was that the Japanese had a trap of their own. High up along the snowy mountainous ridges, the Japanese soldiers were waiting in big dry foxholes with plenty of guns, ammunition, and food. Some of the foxholes even had underground chambers that could hold a dozen men.

To top it off, the Japanese were well hidden by the fog and were further camouflaged in white fur-lined uniforms — coats, vests, mittens, and boots.

"The Japanese had dug in well," said Eugene Burns, a *New York Times* newspaper reporter on the scene. "Their mountainside positions were prepared so that they offered the maximum protection and the best field of fire through which troops had to go."

On this day, the fog was the ally of the Japanese and an enemy to the U.S. soldiers. The Americans

American soldiers in a trench, firing back at Japanese soldiers on a hillside hidden in the fog

couldn't see the Japanese, but the Japanese could see the Americans. They watched and waited in the fog with their guns pointed at the U.S. soldiers down below.

"The Japanese had dug tunnels for strong points that we couldn't see through the fog," said Sergeant William S. Jones. "They sniped at us every time the fog lifted. As soon as we concentrated our fire back where we thought they were firing from, they pulled back into the tunnels. They were also using smokeless powder, and that made it hard to see where they were firing from."

As the American combat troops tried to move

U.S. soldiers cooking on Attu

forward and upward, the Japanese pinned them down, stopping their advance. When an American finally caught a glimpse of the Japanese, the Japanese soldiers would disappear into the fog.

By the next day, forty-four American soldiers were dead. But that was only the beginning.

By May 14, 1943, on the fourth day of the battle for Attu, little progress had been made, and the U.S. soldiers were out of food and ravenous. On the first day, Lieutenant Anthony Brannen piloted a B-24 and tried to air-drop food and ammunition by parachutes to Captain Willoughby, but the wind blew the supplies into a crevasse and the troops couldn't get to them. He tried again the following day, but crashed into a mountain and was killed. Since then, the planes were socked in by the fog and hadn't been able to drop supplies. No one — with the exception of Eric — was daring enough to fly in it.

The American troops were vulnerable, but the fog was both an enemy and ally. At this point in time, if the Japanese had been able to launch an air attack from their military base on Paramushir Island in the Kuriles, the American troops would have been wiped out.

Of the 12,500 American soldiers on Attu, hundreds

U.S. soldier being treated for trench foot

were suffering from frostbite and trench foot within the first few days.

When the temperature was less than fifty-five degrees Farenheit, as it was in the Aleutians, it only took a few hours for the soldiers' wet feet to develop trench foot. This excruciating condition caused their feet to swell, damaging the nerves and muscles. Each step caused extreme pain, and some of the men were forced to crawl on their hands and knees.

When their feet were finally dry and warmed, the skin turned red or blue and blisters bubbled up. Some got infected, causing gangrene to set in, which destroyed the tissue and often resulted in their feet being amputated.

•   •   •

It wasn't until May 16, 1943, six days after the U.S. troops landed, that they finally had a breakthrough. When the sun finally set around 10:30 P.M., Colonel Frank L. Culin and his Company B of the Seventh Infantry climbed the rugged ridge on Davis Hill and attacked the Japanese head-on.

U.S. soldiers waiting for a mortar shell to explode

For several bloody hours they fought in hand-to-hand combat, finally forcing the Japanese to retreat. The Americans now had control of Holtz Valley. Company B of the Seventh Infantry would be awarded the Presidential Unit Citation for their fearless and valiant fighting.

For the next ten days, the fighting between the Americans and Japanese was brutal. Slowly, the Japanese were being pushed back toward the main Japanese camp in Chichagof Harbor. The U.S. plan was working, until May 26, 1943, when it came to a standstill.

For two days, on the snowy and rocky ridge called

Fish Hook, Company K of the Thirty-Second Infantry had been trying to break through the Japanese line of defense. If the Americans succeeded, it would be the last push needed to send the Japanese into the final trap — but the Japanese weren't giving an inch.

Whenever the Japanese were cornered, they fought harder. They were strategically positioned in a cliff above the American soldiers. From their trench in an overhang, they fired their guns and threw grenades, pinning down the American soldiers below.

Crouched behind a rock, with bullets whistling past his head, was twenty-three-year-old Private Joseph P. Martinez. Joe was a man of few words. Before joining the army ten months earlier, he had worked on a farm, growing and harvesting sugar beets in a small Colorado town. Now he was armed with a Browning automatic rifle (BAR) and had a bag of grenades hanging from his shoulder.

The situation seemed hopeless. The Japanese position was too strong. It didn't look like the Americans would ever break through.

Suddenly, Joe stood up in the line of fire. He ran up the crest of the cliff through a hail of gunfire and positioned himself on a rock that protruded from the edge. He fired away at the Japanese soldiers, continuing to kill one soldier after another.

"And then we heard it," said Sergeant Earl L. Marks. "A kind of crack and thoomp!"

Joe was hit. He fell backward, but no one could help him because the Japanese were pummeling them with grenades. After about half a dozen grenades were tossed, it was silent.

The fight was over for now, and by killing five Japanese soldiers, Joe had single-handedly cleared a section of Fish Hook, allowing the U.S. soldiers to finally advance.

From a distance, Earl could see Joe. He looked dead, but then his hand moved. Earl and Sergeant Glen Swearingen crawled over the cold ground toward him.

"He had been hit through the edge of his helmet," said Earl.

Glen took off his jacket and placed it under Joe. Joe moaned in agony, but there weren't any stretchers to move him to a field hospital.

That night the air was bitterly cold and snow was falling, but Company K armed themselves with a newly delivered stash of grenades and made their way up the crest to the pass where the Japanese were holding their defensive position.

"We let the grenades sizzle for about three counts and then tossed them over," said Earl.

The exploding grenades lit up the pass, and the Japanese were quick to throw grenades back. A hushed silence suddenly fell, and the fighting ceased.

When morning came the Japanese were gone; they had retreated, and Joe was dead. He would receive the Medal of Honor posthumously, the highest honor awarded for heroism. Joe was the first private to earn the medal in World War II and the only one to earn it in the Battle of Attu.

Two days later, on May 28, 1943, the Japanese were surrounded by American soldiers who were now high up in the ridges looking down on them in Chichagof Valley. Eric and his bomber pilots had flown in and demolished the Japanese camp and the village of Attu. The Japanese had little food, ammunition, or supplies left, and no one was going to come to help them. The fleet of submarines that was sent to evacuate them couldn't break through the U.S. naval blockade.

A PBY was sent to fly over the Japanese camp and drop thousands of leaflets with instructions for the Japanese to surrender. The Japanese were trapped, but their leader, Colonel Yasuyo Yamasaki, had a plan — one that American military historians considered brilliant. It was the one tactic that could reverse the battle, turning the tide in Japan's favor.

Colonel Yamasaki ordered all documents to be burned and called a meeting of his troops.

"We are planning a successful annihilation of the enemy," he told them.

At the meeting, listening to Colonel Yamasaki give his orders, was the quiet and studious Dr. Paul Nobuo Tatsuguchi. Paul was born and raised in Hiroshima, Japan, but had been educated in America, just like his father

Japanese soldiers on Attu during the winter of 1943

and his older brother. He studied at Pacific Union College and Loma Linda University School of Medicine in California, where he earned his medical degree in 1938.

Paul loved America. He was filled with good memories of traveling to Yosemite National Park, where he'd proposed to his wife, Taeko. He and Taeko planned on returning to America with their two young daughters after the war.

Paul was a devout Christian and had gone back to Japan after graduating to do missionary work for the Seventh-Day Adventist Church. In Japan, Paul worked at the Tokyo Sanitarium, which specialized in cases of tuberculosis.

Paul was drafted into the Japanese army, but he did not believe in war. It was against his Christian faith. However, he wanted to save lives, and he could do that as a doctor in the war. So when he received his orders from Colonel Yamasaki to "tend to" his wounded patients he felt sickened and at odds with himself.

As Paul made his way to the new field hospital through the deep muddy trenches, which snaked for two miles across the valley, he felt his stomach aching from hunger. Food had been so scarce for the past week that the Japanese had begun stealing it from one another.

Paul carried his medical bags into the field hospital. Inside his bags were his diary, a used copy of *Gray's Anatomy*, and his Bible. Stuck between the pages of the Bible was a photo of his wife and three-year-old daughter, Misako. He hadn't yet seen his baby daughter, Mutsuko.

Following Colonel Yamasaki's orders, Paul "tended

to" the wounded patients in the field hospital. He gave the helpless and incapacitated patients lethal shots of morphine and the lucid patients hand grenades. Today, Paul wasn't trying to heal their wounds or save their lives. He'd been ordered to kill them.

Paul and the other Japanese doctors were saving the patients' honor by helping them follow the *bushido* code. Killing the wounded patients prevented the shame of being captured by the Americans and becoming prisoners of war.

In his diary, which he began when the Americans first landed on Attu, Paul wrote his final thoughts:

"The last assault is to be carried out. All the patients in the hospital were made to commit suicide. Only 33 years of living and I am to die here. I have no regrets. Banzai to the Emperor. I am grateful I have kept the peace of my soul which Edict bestowed upon me. At 1800 took care of all the patients with grenades. Good-bye Taeko, my beloved wife, who has loved to the last. Until we meet again, grant you Godspeed."

By three A.M., when it was still dark, Colonel Yamasaki and his soldiers armed themselves with the few guns and grenades they had, some of which had been captured from the American soldiers. Those who didn't have a gun, attached a bayonet to a stick. Using up the last of their rice supply, each soldier was given two baseball-sized rice balls. If they needed more food, they were told to steal it from the pockets of their dead comrades.

Like ninja warriors, they moved silently through the darkness and shifting fog. The American soldiers standing guard at their camp in the middle of Chichagof Valley didn't hear or see them coming. The Japanese plunged their bayonets into the American soldiers. They had broken through the American front line and quickly charged ahead, killing several sleeping men in a nearby foxhole.

With their guns loaded and bayonets drawn, they charged a camp of unsuspecting Americans who were asleep in their tents. It was a full-fledged banzai attack.

"We die — you die, too!" the Japanese screamed, over and over again.

The Japanese mission was to capture several artillery guns and turn them on the Americans. And, while the banzai attack created mayhem, the Japanese soldiers planned to raid the Americans' supply of food and ammunition. But first, they needed to get to Engineer Hill, located at the north end of the eastern ridgeline of Massacre Valley. It was where the Americans had stashed the supplies for the infantry.

Approximately eight hundred Japanese soldiers swarmed into the base of Engineer Hill and surrounded the Americans. Captain Willoughby was attacked while trying to sleep in his foxhole. "I got a machine-gun bullet across my face and then a hand grenade came into the hole with me. It put some hunks of heavy metal in me, tore up my chest and arm."

The attack raged on for several hours. In a hospital tent, the wounded Americans were piling up. Fighting could be heard in the distance as Captain Charles H. Yellin tried to save the wounded. Suddenly, machine-gun bullets ripped through the tent and bayonets tore it wide open. Outside, the screaming Japanese pulled the pins out of their grenades and threw them at the men inside. Captain Yellin survived.

"I was on the left flank when they came at us," said Technician Fifth Grade Victor J. Unrein, who was shot near his kidney. "There must have been six or seven hundred of them in the attack."

When the morning sun finally lit up the sky, it

revealed the bloodshed. Everyone was either dead or wounded from bullets and shrapnel.

In the meantime, American soldiers fled the scene, racing up Engineer Hill to alert the others. Having no time to put on their shoes, some ran through the icy cold and snow barefooted.

There weren't any combat soldiers on Engineer Hill; they were all engineers and bulldozer drivers as well as cooks, supply haulers, and staff officers. But they grabbed their weapons and got ready to fire. They managed to fend off the Japanese until the infantry advanced and pinned the Japanese down.

The banzai attack was over by mid afternoon, but not the killing. By nightfall, Colonel Yamasaki was dead, and the five hundred remaining Japanese soldiers honored the *bushido* code: Death before dishonor.

"All of a sudden, you could see the Japanese jump and fall down," said Thomas A. Quintrell, an army officer. "It was their grenades — they were killing themselves."

Ordered to kill themselves instead of surrendering, the Japanese pulled the pins of their grenades, armed them with a tap to their helmet, and held them to their head, chest, or stomach.

Mass suicide of the Japanese soldiers on Attu

Lying dead near a field-hospital tent was Dr. Paul Tatsuguchi. It was unclear how he met his fate, but it is believed that he tried to surrender. However, the U.S. soldiers did not hear him, and they shot him.

Lying near Paul's lifeless body were his medical bags. An American soldier found them and brought them to Dr. J. Lawrence Whitaker, a battalion surgeon in the Thirty-Second Infantry, Seventh Division, who was working in the nearby hospital station. When Lawrence looked through the medical bags, he found Paul's secondhand *Gray's Anatomy*. When he opened it and looked at the inside cover he was shocked to see the names Ed Lee and Paul Tatsuguchi.

Later, his shock turned to sadness when Paul's diary was found and a startling truth was revealed. Ed Lee had been a classmate of Paul's and Lawrence's in medical school. Lawrence had bought this copy of *Gray's Anatomy* from Ed Lee and, in his senior year, had sold it to Paul, who was a junior at the time. Lawrence and Paul actually knew each other from school.

The fight for Attu was a costly war in human lives. It was one of the biggest mass suicides in World War II. For every ten Japanese soldiers who were killed, seven American soldiers were killed or wounded. There were more than 15,000 U.S. soldiers on Attu, and of those, 549 were killed in action, 1,148 were wounded, and 1,200 had severe injuries from the cold. By the end, 2,650 Japanese soldiers and civilians were dead, leaving only 29 alive. The living Japanese were cooks, hospital orderlies, and civilian laborers who became prisoners of war. No Japanese officers survived.

Not expecting any of their men to be taken alive, the Japanese had not been told what to do if they were captured. As a result, the Japanese prisoners were very obedient to authority. Castner's Cutthroat Major William Verbeck was a witness to the interrogation of the first Japanese prisoners captured on Attu.

"The Japanese prisoner ... has never been told not to talk in event of capture," he reported. "Because the possibility of capture is never considered by the enemy. As a result, this well-disciplined Japanese soldier obeys orders and answers any questions we direct to him."

When questioned, the Japanese prisoners said they did not kill themselves because they were either lost or had no grenades. All of them said they didn't want their families to know they were still alive.

Japanese POWs

"I'd like to go back to Japan," said one Japanese POW. "But if I go back I'd be a disgrace to the folks so I don't know what to do. Under such circumstances we are theoretically dead, so if there is anything I can do to work for the United States I'd like to do that."

On May 31, 1943, the Japanese government issued a statement about the Battle of Attu: "It is assumed the entire Japanese force has preferred death to dishonor."

The battle for Attu was over, and so were the lives of thousands of men.

CHAPTER 8
The Surprise Attack

JULY 26, 1943. KISKA, ALASKA, AFTER MIDNIGHT.

When the Japanese guards, who were on duty at an outpost at Vega Point on Kiska, looked out across the horizon, they were perplexed. It wasn't because they could actually see the moon and the stars twinkling in the cloudless night sky. Nor was it the surprise that the fog had lifted and the weather had cleared. What confounded the Japanese guards were the flashing lights that were illuminating the dark sky like fireworks.

To them, it looked and sounded like a battle was raging out at sea, but they didn't see how that was possible. They knew the Japanese ships and submarines were steering clear of the American naval blockade that surrounded the Japanese troops on Kiska.

At the same time, deep inside an underground tunnel at the Kiska naval headquarters, the Japanese

Entrance to one of the Japanese tunnels

telecommunications intelligence unit was listening in on the U.S. Navy's radio transmissions. One of the people listening was Karl Kasukabe, the interpreter who had been stationed at Attu. Karl had arrived on Kiska when the Imperial Military Headquarters transferred the troops in Attu to Kiska. Karl had been on Kiska ever since, and he'd fared pretty well until about two months ago. It was on June 10, 1943, during an air raid, that a bomb was dropped on Karl's barracks. Karl was buried alive and knocked unconscious. He was rescued but his left leg and hip were crushed. Despite his severe injuries, Karl worked diligently translating and decoding American radio transmissions and weather code telegrams. The Japanese knew the Americans were coming to fight for Kiska any day now, and an unshakable feeling of doom weighed heavily on their hearts and minds.

Inside of an underground Japanese bunkhouse

Tonight, Karl's job was made easier because the Americans were transmitting messages in plain English. Since Karl didn't have to waste time decoding messages, it wasn't long before he heard something very interesting. In fact, it was critical to the entire Japanese unit on Kiska. He immediately alerted the others.

The Japanese troops on Kiska may have been surrounded by an American naval blockade, but they had one more trick up their sleeves. And the magician who would make it happen was Rear Admiral Masatomi Kimura.

•   •   •

Three days later, on July 29, 1943, the USS *Zeilin* left the port of San Francisco and headed west. Crammed onboard were three thousand mountain soldiers. They were the U.S. Army's Eighty-Seventh Mountain Infantry, Tenth Division, an elite group of top-notch skiers and intrepid rock climbers.

Belowdecks, it was a tight squeeze with eleven soldiers sharing one cabin furnished with narrow bunk beds. Each soldier carried an eighty-five pound backpack and was outfitted with blanket-lined pants, skis, snowshoes, goose-down sleeping bags, camping and climbing gear, and weapons.

When they left San Francisco, none of the soldiers knew where they were going — it was top secret. They could only guess.

When they weren't on duty, the soldiers passed the time playing cards and telling stories, but when the ship made a sharp turn to the north, they knew they were in trouble. They were headed to the American military base in Adak and would be sent to Kiska to fight the Japanese.

The Tenth Mountain Division had never been in combat before, and everyone knew the battle for Attu had been a bloodbath.

"We were all scared stiff," said Lieutenant Roger W. Eddy, a Tenth Mountain Division soldier who was a world-class skier and Yale-educated farmer.

The American soldiers knew the Japanese forces were entrenched and ready to attack. The mountain soldiers heard a rumor that 90 percent of them were expected to die at the hands of the Japanese.

On the ship, they tried to enjoy their last moments by listening to popular music on the shortwave radio, but it didn't help. Tokyo Rose interrupted their program. She taunted them with a warning: "All you boys on the *Zeilin* headed for Kiska Island, there's a big surprise waiting there for you."

Kiska Island was shrouded in the thick pea-soup fog on August 15, 1943, when the first wave of 34,426 U.S. Army and Navy soldiers, which included 5,300 from the Thirteenth Canadian Infantry Brigade, began landing on the shores. The tide was low, exposing hazardous rocks, while the men were taken ashore one boat at a time through the icy water.

The first to go in were Castner's Cutthroats, led by Major Verbeck. They landed on Gertrude Cove, with the hope of tricking the enemy into thinking they were the main landing force. From Gertrude

U.S. and Canadian soldiers landing on Kiska

Cove, the Cutthroats were to kill the enemy as they hiked across to Quisling Cove, where the actual landing was taking place.

On the northwest side of Kiska, the mountain soldiers were to follow a small scouting party. The mountain soldiers had to not only scale the side of the steep cliff, but also cut stairs into it for the combat soldiers who would follow.

Waiting nervously to board a boat that would take him ashore in the second wave of landings was Private George F. Earle, a soldier with the Tenth Mountain Division. George was a Yale graduate who had worked as an art teacher before he joined the army after Pearl Harbor was attacked. He was recruited for the division because he was a fantastic skier.

George wasn't the only artist in the Tenth. His good friend, Lieutenant Wilfred J. Funk, was a sculptor. Wilfred was an expert mountain climber, and he combined his love for art and climbing when he helped Gutzon Borglum sculpt Mt. Rushmore. Wilfred enjoyed telling the story about how he dangled from a rope off Teddy Roosevelt's mustache and Abraham Lincoln's lower lip.

The night before the landing on Kiska, George and Wilfred weren't the only soldiers thinking about death. And no one's mind was eased when they were each given a white mattress cover to carry in their packs. At first, they didn't know what it was for, and they were shocked to learn it would be used as a shroud to cover their dead bodies.

Some sat down and wrote their final farewell letter to their families. Everyone was served a steak dinner with french fries and cake, but most soldiers couldn't eat because they were worried sick. Afterward, the chaplain read a prayer. The Tenth went to bed at eleven P.M., and those who managed to catch a few winks of sleep were awakened at five

A.M. to the blaring sound of loudspeakers. It was time for the first wave of soldiers to land on Kiska.

Landing on the shore at around noon that day was Corporal Leo J. "Oley" Kohlman of the Tenth. He was in charge of keeping everyone supplied — from the underwear and socks the soldiers wore to the machine guns they slung over their shoulders. He was also an expert on both American and Japanese weapons, and he instructed the soldiers how to fire everything from machine guns to rocket launchers.

As Leo slogged his way through the sandy beach toward the steep cliff he would have to climb, he suddenly stopped in his tracks. Four soldiers were returning from the battle high up on the ridge. They were carrying a stretcher. As they passed by, Leo saw a bloody, dead soldier. Leo, who was never at a loss for words, was speechless after witnessing their group's first casualty of war.

Later in the afternoon, up on the craggy ridge, the men tried to dig foxholes, but shoveling the rocky terrain proved tough and the foxholes were shallow. They would have to make do with these and crouch down to take cover from flying bullets and grenades.

As the hurricane-force winds blew, the thick fog made things shimmer like a reflection in a pool of wavy water, tricking the eye into seeing the form of a person in what was, in fact, just a pile of rocks. Plodding through this tricky layer of fog was George Earle. He was trekking down a slope with an operations officer, trying to gather information on their positions on the front line, when they came upon a soldier lying on the ground. The soldier's pants were drenched in blood. He'd been shot in the thigh, and he couldn't climb up the ridge.

"He assured us that he had killed the Jap[anese] who had shot him," said George. "He had seen him clearly and close up and watched him fall."

But no one could find the Japanese soldier's body.

That night there was fog, rain, and wind as the men huddled in their muddy foxholes, hoping that the Japanese weren't coming to slay them with their bayonets. The sounds of tracer bullets whistling and the *ack-ack-ack* of machine-gun fire were heard throughout the seemingly endless night. By morning there were a total of fifteen dead soldiers on Kiska. One of them was Wilfred Funk, the once-promising sculptor. He'd been shot several times.

"He died leading a heroic charge to save that command post that was out of position. . . . He was a friend from the inside out," said George.

As the wounded and the dead were carried down

the steep and slippery ridge, a troubling observation was made. There weren't any dead Japanese soldiers — anywhere.

Soon after, Technician Fifth Class Robert W. Parker, whose job in the Tenth was intelligence and reconnaissance, was sent out with his unit to find the Japanese. Their mission was to determine if the Japanese troops had moved to the southern side of the island.

"We thought we were going into the jaws of death," said Robert. "None of us was sure whether we'd ever climb back up those hills."

Before long they came upon a Japanese artillery installation, and what they found was more disturbing than they would have ever guessed. It was deserted, revealing the awful truth.

"There weren't any Japanese at all on Kiska Island," said Robert.

The Allied soldiers had been shooting at one another. In all, seventeen Americans and four Canadians were killed and fifty were wounded. The causes were friendly fire or booby traps rigged by the Japanese.

"We were exhausted, disgusted, and ashamed," said Roger Eddy. "And we knew we'd done all the killing ourselves."

Disarmed Japanese booby trap

• • •

The Japanese escape from Kiska began after midnight on July 26, 1943, three weeks before the American and Canadian troops landed on Kiska. When the Japanese guards saw the flashing lights that were illuminating the midnight sky like fireworks, they did not know they were coming from American ships. And they did not know that these ships had been ordered to withdraw from the naval blockade to find a Japanese fleet that had been spotted on their radar screen as a series of seven blips, or pips as they were called back then.

Although they had been alerted about the order by Karl Kasukabe, who was listening in on the American radio transmissions, the Japanese didn't know which fleet the Americans were chasing because they knew that Rear Admiral Masatomi Kimura and his rescue fleet were waiting five hundred miles south of Kiska. The American ships firing their guns on the horizon thought they were engaged in a battle with a Japanese fleet. It turned out the Americans were firing at a "phantom fleet."

To this day, no one knows for sure what the Americans saw on the radar screen that made them think Japanese ships were in the area. It is suspected that the radar pips leading to the Battle of the Pips were a flock of birds.

Karl also learned from the radio transmission that after the phantom battle the American fleet planned to refuel. This gave the Japanese ten to twelve hours to put their escape plan into action.

The Japanese knew that in order for their plan to work, they would need a thick blanket of fog to hide them, so they monitored Russian and American radio weather reports. Using these and Japanese weather

Japanese weather station on Kiska

forecasts, the Kiska weatherman determined that, despite the unusually clear weather they'd been experiencing, the fog would roll back in on July 29. Although fog is never easy to predict, this time he was right.

Admiral Kimura and his fleet of destroyers and cruisers stealthily approached Kiska Island by taking the most dangerous route, strategizing that it was the least likely route to encounter American submarines and ships. A radio beacon guided him into Kiska Bay, where Karl and the rest of the Japanese unit were waiting on the beach.

Within fifty-five minutes, five thousand Japanese were evacuated from Kiska, successfully escaping under cover of fog without a single casualty.

A month later, on August 21, President Roosevelt and Canadian prime minister W. L. Mackenzie King issued a joint statement announcing the end of the Aleutian War. The navy also issued a statement, which revealed to the American public for the first time that on August 15, U.S. and Canadian troops had landed on Kiska.

"No Japanese have been found," the U.S. Navy stated. "There were indications of [a] recent hasty evacuation of the Japanese garrison. . . . It is not known how the Japanese got away, but it is possible that enemy surface ships were able to reach Kiska under cover of heavy fogs that have been prevalent."

On the same day, the Japanese government announced that the Japanese army and naval forces had been transferred from Kiska to a new post over two and a half weeks before and that the operation was met "without enemy interference."

Radio Tokyo also broadcasted the news that the

Japanese forces had not been on Kiska since the end of July.

The U.S. Navy issued a second statement contradicting the Japanese reports that the Japanese hadn't been on Kiska for over two weeks, stating "light antiaircraft fire was encountered" in an air raid on Kiska on August 13.

Three days later the Japanese government announced that the ghosts of the dead Japanese soldiers on Attu must have caused the American ships to fire at one another, and had fought the American soldiers on Kiska. An Australian newspaper, the *Sydney Morning Herald*, picked up the story and published it as "Ghosts Fight Allies."

Even though the Aleutian War was over, the Tenth Mountain Division remained on Kiska until December 1943 to sweep the island for land mines and booby traps that the Japanese had rigged before they left. One day, deep inside an underground tunnel, mountain soldier Private Sherman L. Smith found a Japanese flag. He quickly discovered that it was attached to a bomb. Wasting no time, he fearlessly cut the wires leading to the explosives and successfully defused it.

When Sherman looked the flag over, he noticed Japanese writing all over it. He folded the flag up and put it in his pack. He wanted to keep it as a souvenir.

What Sherman didn't know, at the time, was that on top of the flag the Japanese writing said, LIVE LONG KASUKABE!

CHAPTER 9
Ghost Towns

Mother and daughter being evacuated from St. George Island

At four o'clock in the morning, the eighty-three Atkan evacuees were transferred from the USS *Delarof* onto a massive red freight barge. Parents held their children tightly in their arms as they walked carefully down the wooden gangplank. The Atkans, along with the Aleuts from the Pribilof Islands of St. George and St. Paul, had already traveled fifteen hundred miles, which is

159

about halfway across the continental United States. It was a grueling voyage.

"We did not travel for speed," said Anatoly Lekanof, who was eleven years old and had been evacuated from St. George. "They . . . traveled to make sure that the enemy was not below us in a submarine. We voyaged in a zigzag manner. We would have a periodic drill — at unannounced odd hours — to go out on deck with our lifejackets to see how fast we could get out in case we had to abandon ship."

The *Delarof*, which was designed to hold 300 people, already had 560 Aleuts from Atka and the Pribilof Islands onboard. The Aleuts were crammed down in the ship's hold, the area belowdecks. There were bunk beds and some mattresses on the floor to sleep on, but there was only one toilet and sink. And there weren't any showers for bathing.

"People were packed together in the bowels of the ship. People were lying around, not moving. It was dark like a dungeon," said Alexandra Gromoff, who was fifteen years old and had been evacuated from the Pribilof island of St. Paul.

In the overcrowded hold, it was wet and drafty, creating the perfect environment for a serious outbreak of "ship's cold," a flulike infection, to strike the passengers. There wasn't any extra room to quarantine the sick, and the infection spread quickly. Making matters worse, the doctor from St. George would not treat those from the island, fearing for his own health. When Haretina Kochutin, who was nine months pregnant and very ill, went into labor, the doctor from St. George refused to help her.

In the dark, drafty, and infectious hold, Haretina delivered a baby girl and named her Susan "Dela" Kochutin. Three days later, Dela died from bronchial pneumonia. At the midnight funeral, the sky was a fiery red and orange as the summer sun finally began to set. Everyone onboard, including the doctor who had refused to help, stood in silence. Captain Gene Downey turned off the *Delarof*'s engine, and, in the hushed silence, they heard a splash of water when Dela's bundled body hit the lonely sea.

When the people from Atka were told to board the red freight barge that stunk of rotting fish, no one complained. Everyone was relieved to be off the *Delarof* and on a barge that would take them to a new place to call home.

The Aleuts from the Pribilof Islands had already been dropped off the day before at Funter Bay on Admiralty Island. Now it was the Atkans' turn. They were going to be settled on the southern tip of Admiralty Island at Killisnoo, fifty miles south of Funter Bay, and a few hours away by boat. The only people nearby were in Angoon, where the Kootznoowoo Tlingit tribe of American Indians lived. The nearest cities were Juneau (fifty-five miles away) and Sitka (forty-one miles away), but they would have no way of getting there on their own.

Everyone was now safely out of the war zone and out of harm's way. Or so they thought.

Alongside the red barge, there was a ship carrying Governor Gruening and Claude Hirst, the general superintendent of the Alaska Indian Service. Mr. Hirst and his department had been in charge of selecting Funter Bay and Killisnoo as evacuation camp locales. He and the governor were there to witness the evacuees' "safe" arrival at Killisnoo.

Seeing the governor and general superintendent nearby, Ruby Magee, dressed in a pink sweater and blue pants, lined the children up on the barge and led them in a rip-roaring sing-along. Their finale was "God Bless America," which they sang with unbridled glee. Everyone clapped their hands,

Ruby and Ralph Magee

and Governor Gruening, Mr. Hirst, and others in the audience tossed the children some pennies to show their appreciation.

As the barge arrived at the rocky shores of Killisnoo, the exhausted Atkans were happy their long and punishing journey was finally coming to an end. That is, until they saw their final destination.

"When we first got here it felt good 'cause we had been on the boat for so long," said Alice Snigaroff Petrivelli, who was twelve years old. "And to breathe the fresh air, to smell the trees and roses."

For most Aleuts, this was the first time they'd ever seen a tree, with the exception of the occasional Christmas tree purchased from a mail-order catalog.

However, for many Aleuts the trees were an unsettling sight — a towering reminder that they were far away from their beloved home, the treeless Aleutian Islands.

But the newfangled trees would become the least

of their worries after they got a good look at the camp. When everyone saw the buildings they were supposed to live in, their hearts sank.

"There were some very old flimsy buildings that had belonged to a fish meal factory," said Ralph Magee, who, along with his wife, Ruby, was now in charge of managing the evacuee camp.

The camp at Killisnoo was a rotting cannery that had been closed down twenty-four years before, after a fire destroyed the nearby village that had never been rebuilt. The Atkans were to live in the deserted and dilapidated cottages and dormitories where the cannery workers had once lived during the warmer summer months.

"We were told to fix them over to live in 'for the duration,'" said Ralph.

The repairs needed were not minor. The buildings and sidewalks were made of wood that had mostly rotted over the years, and the roofs provided little shelter from the elements.

The evacuee camp didn't have the basic necessities needed to live. There was one pump for springwater, but the water was contaminated and needed to be boiled before drinking. Making matters worse, not everyone had a stove to boil the

Children at the only water faucet at Killisnoo

water. If they wanted safe water to drink, they were going to have to dig a well themselves.

There was no indoor plumbing, so the eighty-three Atkans would have to use the three decaying outhouses until they built more. And if they wanted to bathe, there was only one bathtub in the entire camp.

The run-down buildings were wired for electricity, but the unsafe wiring would put the Aleuts at risk of starting a fire if they used it.

It wasn't any better for the Aleuts from the Pribilof Islands who were dropped off at Funter Bay, or the people from St. George who were to live in an abandoned gold mining camp.

There was no individual housing or rooms for the families to live in. Instead, there were a few buildings with a large room where everyone would have to sleep together. To gain some privacy, the Aleuts hung wool blankets from the ceiling to partition an eight- by ten-foot space in the room where eight to ten people slept on the floor.

"We all slept like sardines. Just mattress alongside mattress, and just kind of head-to-foot," Anatoly said. "Not everybody's head alongside each other in case one didn't want to hear another's snoring."

Their sleeping space was more crowded than a prison cell at Alcatraz in San Fransisco Bay, which was notorious for its punishing living conditions. A prison cell at Alcatraz was five by nine feet and was equipped with a bed, toilet, and sink with running water and electricity. And there was only one prisoner living in each cell at Alcatraz. At Funter Bay, the partitioned space was the equivalent to packing four or five people in a prison cell at Alcatraz, but with none of the basic amenities.

At Funter Bay there was no indoor plumbing

or running water. The one usable outhouse on the end of the pier emptied directly into the bay, contaminating the water. Because the water from the bay wasn't safe to drink, the Aleuts had to carry bucketfuls from a nearby stream and in winter, break through the ice to get to it.

In the coming weeks, all of the remaining Aleuts were evacuated from the Aleutian Islands. The Aleuts in the villages of Nikolski, Kashega, Makushin, Biorka, Unalaska, and Akutan were whisked away from their homes at a moment's notice. All of the evacuees were only allowed to bring one bag of personal belongings each and were dropped off at camps that had horrible conditions.

When Chief William Zaharoff of Unalaska saw the conditions of Burnet Inlet, he fired off a telegram to Claude Hirst, whose Alaska Indian Service had picked the place. Chief Zaharoff wrote that "the water is low and not fit to drink," there was no fish or game, and the "houses are not fit to live in." People were already sick within ten days of arriving, and the chief's wife, Mary, was taken to the hospital in Ketchikan because she had become very ill. He asked for a "better place" for the Aleuts to live, but his request was denied.

When the unexpected order came to evacuate the

Aleuts, the Alaska Indian Service was put in charge of finding them a place to live. There was no time to spare, as hundreds of Aleuts would be arriving in a matter of days, and they would need food, clothing, and shelter, at the very least.

Without any preparation or contingency plans in place, the Indian Service officials made hasty decisions. They wanted to keep the Aleuts from each community together, so the Aleuts from Atka would be in one camp, and the Aleuts from St. Paul in another, and so forth. The choices were limited, and they decided to move the Aleuts into ghost towns — knowing full well that they were uninhabitable but figuring the Aleuts could make repairs and improvements.

The Aleuts were highly skilled carpenters and more than capable of fixing up the buildings. They were, after all, well adept at surviving in one of the harshest environments in the world and had done so for nine thousand years. Nonetheless, the critical difference in the camps was that they were completely empty-handed — they lacked the tools, lumber, boats, guns, fishing poles, beds, sheets, blankets, food, or medicines needed to survive in this unfamiliar environment: The Atkans had arrived with only the clothes on their backs.

In their first winter, there were record-breaking cold temperatures combined with blizzards.

Their food supply froze solid, and meat was in short supply.

"They missed the reindeer and sea lions of Atka more than anything else," Ruby Magee said. "Deer were hard to get, and little to them when they were found. Yes, the people were plenty homesick for Atka."

Cold, hungry, and sick, the Aleuts had not been given any medical supplies, and at Killisnoo a doctor and nurse only came to help one time, shortly after they first arrived, and never returned. Soon, people started dying at an alarming rate. The most vulnerable were the children and the elders.

"It was a rather hard winter on Killisnoo," said Ralph Magee. "Many of the older people died. We did our best to keep up the morale."

In the Aleut community, the elders are respected and held in high regard for their wisdom and knowledge of the customs, culture, and survival skills, which they share and hand down to the younger members of the community. When an elder dies, a piece of the Aleut way of life dies, too.

Like the Aleut elders, the children were also vulnerable to sickness and death, particularly babies.

However, school-aged children who were allowed to attend the Wrangell Institute, a government boarding school for American Indians, Eskimos, and Aleuts, escaped the hardships endured by the rest of their families who remained in the evacuee camps.

At this time, schools were segregated, and native Alaskans weren't allowed to go to schools with white children. It was also common practice in Alaskan towns to post NO NATIVES signs on the doors and windows of stores and restaurants. In movie theaters, the seating was divided into sections for white people and sections for natives; they weren't allowed to sit together. If anyone did, the native risked getting arrested and thrown in jail.

When the principal of the Wrangell Institute, Mr. George T. Barrett, came to Funter Bay and asked if any of the children between the ages of twelve and fifteen would like to attend the school, thirty signed up.

"I wanted to go," said Flore Lekanof, Anatoly's older brother. "But I knew a boy over sixteen can't go any farther in school, because, where I come from, the Government Service of Fishing and Wild Life puts them to work."

Flore had to ask for special permission from

Edward Johnston, the superintendent of the sealing business for the Fish and Wildlife Service. Flore was surprised he was allowed to go.

"When I got to the Institute I was homesick. . . . First, I learned to look after myself. Second, I became acquainted with the students. I was soon very happy," said Flore. "I had never thought of attending a high school."

But in May 1943, Flore would be pulled out of school even though he was still recovering from the flu. The Fish and Wildlife Service needed him and all able-bodied Aleut men to harvest the seals in the Pribilof Islands.

The U.S. government had made millions of dollars per year in the sealing industry after they purchased Alaska from Russia. But the Aleuts, who lived on the Pribilof Islands and did all the work, made very little. They were not considered employees of the federal government; instead, they were "wards of the state."

This allowed the Fish and Wildlife Service, the government branch in charge of the sealing industry, to exercise control over them. They were not free to leave the Pribilof Islands unless the Fish and Wildlife Service granted them permission. The Fish and Wildlife Service was also allowed to tell them what language they could speak, where they could live, who they could marry, when they would have to start working, and how much money they would make. In return, the Aleuts of the Pribilofs received housing, food, clothing, medical care, and wages.

Every year, up to 150,000 seal furs were harvested during a ten-week period beginning in June. Before the onset of World War II, an Aleut was given on average seventy cents for a seal skin, but the government made one hundred dollars off each one. It took approximately nine seal skins to make a coat, and they were sold for sixteen hundred dollars (in today's dollars, twenty thousand). For centuries seal fur coats were all the rage and were sold in

Seal skinning on St. Paul Island

fashionable stores in New York, Paris, London, Moscow, and all over the world.

With so much money at stake, and short of men, the Fish and Wildlife Service received permission from General Buckner and the War Department to bring the Aleut men who had seal harvesting skills back into the war zone. Although these seal harvesters would be going home, they would not be allowed to stay in their houses, because the military was using them. Instead, the Aleuts would be living in a bunkhouse.

Leaving the women, children, and older men behind at Funter Bay made the conditions at the camp worse. The supplies to repair the buildings were either slow to arrive or never arrived. The overcrowded conditions and lack of medical care, food, and safe drinking water caused epidemics of the flu, measles, and tuberculosis to spread throughout the camps. With nearly everyone getting sick, it was impossible to improve or even maintain the health conditions.

While the Aleut men were away for the seal harvest, Dr. Bernata Block, director of the Division of Maternal and Child Health and Crippled Children's Services in the Territorial Department of Health, came to inspect Funter Bay. At the time, an epidemic of measles was sweeping through the camp. She was shocked at the "deplorable conditions" she witnessed.

"As we entered the first bunkhouse the odor of human waste was so pungent. . . . The buildings were in total darkness except for a few candles. . . . The overcrowding housing condition is really beyond description. . . . The garbage cans were overflowing; human waste was found next to the doors of the cabins and in the drainage boxes into which dishwater and kitchen waste was to be placed . . . There were numerous flies in many rooms," Dr. Block stated in her report.

During this time, Henry Roden, the attorney general of Alaska, also visited Funter Bay. He immediately sent a letter to Governor Gruening, which said, "I have no language at my command which can adequately describe what I saw. . . . I have seen some tough places in my days in Alaska, but nothing to equal the situation at Funter."

But the conditions did not improve much, and when the Aleut men returned to Funter Bay after the largest harvest of seals in seventy-three years, they caught the measles, too.

By October 1943, the invading Japanese were no

longer in the Aleutians and the seal harvest was over. Yet, the Aleuts were still not allowed to return there, even though white men and women who were not in the military were living in the Aleutians.

It turned out that the mandatory evacuation from the Aleutian Islands did not apply to the white people living there. It only applied to the Aleuts, and if a person was one-eighth Aleut or more, that person had to leave.

In May 1944, the Aleuts from the Pribilof Islands were the first to finally return home, just in time for the seal harvest. It would be almost a full year before the rest of the Aleuts were allowed to return.

When the Aleuts returned to Atka, the remnants of war were still visible. The bullet-ridden PBY was still sunk in a watery grave in Nazan Bay. A deep crater from the Japanese bombing the village was hard to miss, and pockmarks from machine-gun fire scarred the hills.

However, that wasn't the worst of it. When Chief William Dirks went inside his home, he discovered that all of his possessions were gone and his home was stripped of everything — except the bathtub and toilet.

It not only happened to the Atkans, it happened

to all the Aleuts. The American soldiers and sailors who were stationed in their villages had vandalized and stolen their property.

Everything the Aleuts owned was stolen: beds, tables, chairs, sofas, dishes, pots, pans, radios, phonographs, photographs, clothing, and Russian religious icons that were priceless heirlooms. Musical instruments, such as accordions and guitars, were also stolen, and a piano, which was too heavy to move, had all of its keys ripped off. Fishing gear and tackle as well as guns were stolen, making it impossible for the Aleuts to fish or hunt for their food.

Aleut cemetery

An inspector from the navy said in his report on the village of Akutan, "Without exception, all rooms in every building of this village clearly gave convincing evidence of looting and ransacking of the very worst kind."

The Aleuts were home, but now they would have to rebuild their villages. Working with the Alaska Indian Service, the army and navy supplied the building materials needed, and the Aleuts were paid fifty cents an hour to do the work. The government also promised to replace their stolen possessions.

"I tried to pretend it was a dream and this could not happen to me and my dear family," said Bill Cherapankoff on his return to Akutan. "I knew I had to salvage my house for my family. I worked till my hands, bleeding with pain, made the wood red."

The disease and destruction caused by the evacuation of the Aleuts during World War II nearly destroyed them and their culture. And it would be years before they received any reparation.

CHAPTER 10
The Prisoners

SEPTEMBER 17, 1945. OTARU, HOKKAIDO, JAPAN, TWO
WEEKS AFTER JAPAN SURRENDERED AND THREE YEARS
AFTER THE ALEUTS WERE TAKEN FROM ATTU.

On the western coast of Hokkaido Island in Otaru, Japan, near the Shimizu-cho Meiji Shrine, where Japanese devotees worshipped and made offerings to their gods and spirits, there was a wooden house. The house had five rooms that, at one time many years ago, were used by a Shinto priest for an office and living space.

When American bomber pilots flew over this single-story house, they could clearly see the letters *PW* written on top of the roof. These letters alerted the pilots that prisoners of war lived inside the house.

Also inside this shabby house was a big box. And inside this big box were twenty little boxes neatly stacked, one on top of the other. This big box was placed near a trunk containing Russian Orthodox Church books.

It hadn't been difficult fitting all of the little boxes into the one large box. The difficult part had been picking up the charred bone fragments of the dead and trying to fit them into the little boxes. Sometimes the boxes simply weren't big enough for the bones to fit.

Along with the twenty boxes of bones, there were twenty urns of ashes packed inside three military caskets. Three years had passed since the Attuans were captured and brought to Japan, and only about half of them had survived.

One of the worst things for the surviving Attuans was that they were not allowed to bury their dead, so the Attuans held on to their loved ones' remains — the bones that didn't burn and the flesh that turned to ashes during the cremation process. "We kept all our boxes carefully because we wanted to take them home to be buried some day," said Alex Prossoff.

From the beginning of their journey from Attu to Japan, death was almost certain for all of them. When the ship left Attu, it first stopped at Kiska to pick up prisoner of war Charlie House.

For the two-week voyage to Japan, the Attuans

remained in the foul-smelling and uncomfortable hold, without the benefit of fresh air or fresh food. Sickness was rampant.

Charlie helped care for the ailing children, and they called him Doc. However, after the ship finally arrived in Japan, they never saw Charlie again.

Since Charlie was in the U.S. Navy, the Japanese treated him as an enemy, and, as such, they believed they had the right to kill him any time they deemed necessary. When Charlie arrived at a secret naval base near Tokyo, they blindfolded him and told him that if he could see, they would have to shoot him.

From there, they took Charlie to a prison camp near Yokohama called Ofuna, which was dubbed a "torture farm" because beatings were an everyday occurrence for the prisoners. POWs in Japan were not protected by the Geneva conventions.

In 1929, political leaders from forty nations met and signed the Geneva convention, an international law that specifies the humane treatment of prisoners of war. Japan was present at the meeting and signed the agreement. Although Japan had signed this agreement, the Japanese government never ratified it because the military leaders opposed it. They believed it did not apply to them because their soldiers followed the *bushido* code, and would kill themselves to avoid becoming prisoners of war.

As a result, the Japanese disdained anyone who surrendered because, to them, it was a shameful act. So without the protection of the Geneva conventions, POWs in Japanese prison camps were tortured, beaten, starved, denied medical attention, deprived of aid from the Red Cross, and used as slave laborers.

Civilians like the Aleuts, on the other hand, were treated somewhat differently. The Japanese did not call them prisoners. Instead, civilians who were captured by the Japanese were referred to as detainees. As detainees, the Aleuts lived together as a family among the Japanese people instead of being sent to a prison camp. Nevertheless, there were guards who policed their every move, and it wasn't long before they were starving.

When the Aleuts arrived in Japan in September 1942, the country's economy was already feeling the squeeze from the cost of war. There was a shortage of coal, raw materials, and labor.

"When we were there, I used to think Japan must be one of the poorest countries in the whole world," said Alex Prossoff. "In that town of Otaru . . . not one painted house did I see. One house only had a coat of tar. Everyone worked, and worked every day. Young boys and girls worked in the factories near the house where we lived."

Earlier that year, a severe drought had destroyed many of Japan's crops, causing a food shortage and inflated food prices. Sugar, meat, and bread were considered luxury items. And rice, their staple food, had to be rationed.

"At first we did all right because we ate the flour and sugar and fish we brought from Attu," said Alex. "The Jap[anese] gave us only two cups of rice for about ten people a day. When our food was gone we could not buy any more from [the] Jap[anese]. Then we began to get very hungry."

On the first night in Japan, Mike Lokanin's baby daughter, Titiana, was crying for a bottle of milk. Titiana was still too young to eat solid foods. When Mike asked the Japanese guards for milk, they couldn't understand one another. Eventually, Mike realized that there was no milk to give her.

The Aleuts soon learned that they had to adapt to many aspects of the Japanese culture. They were told to take off their shoes before entering their house. At first, they didn't understand why because the house was dirty, but they learned this was a Japanese custom.

When they ate their first meal in Japan, instead of sitting in a chair at a table, the guard instructed them to sit on the floor cross-legged. Eating became problematic for the Aleuts when they were given chopsticks. Like many Americans at the time, the Aleuts didn't know how to use chopsticks because they were accustomed to knives, forks, and spoons. So, as soon as the guards looked away or were busy talking to one another, the Aleuts shoveled their food into their mouths with their hands.

To sleep, they were given futons and tatami mats instead of the Western-style beds they were used to. "Pillows were also given to us, and they were very hard, but we did not complain," said Olean Golodoff, the mother of seven children, all of whom were prisoners in Japan.

All of the Aleuts, including the children, were expected to learn how to speak Japanese.

"The Jap[anese] said they would kill us if we didn't," said Alex.

Like the American soldiers who were prisoners of war, the Attuans were beaten by the Japanese guards.

"Sometimes we were beaten and our women whipped," said Alex.

"The less I remember the better," said John Golodoff, who was Olean's son and fifteen years old when he was taken to Japan. John was beaten for not working fast enough.

Angelina Hodikoff, who was Chief Mike Hodikoff's sixteen-year-old daughter, had scars from the beatings she received. One time a Japanese guard threw a stone at her, wounding her, because she had stopped working.

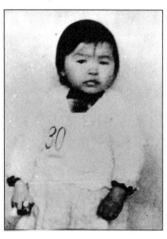

Elizabeth Golodoff Kudrin at 18 months old. She was taken to Japan in 1942 and didn't return to the United States until age 3.

Within the first month of arriving, the Aleuts were put to work in a mine digging bentonite, a type of white clay that had many different uses, out of the side of a mountain. The clay was then mashed with sticks so it could dry in the sun. When it finally turned into a powder, they turned on a machine with a fan that blew the powder through a pipe into a large hole in the ground.

Mike's job was to keep the powder from plugging

up the pipe. There was a large piece of canvas over the hole, and Mike was kept inside the hole until it filled up with powder. When the hole got full, he tapped on the canvas, and they would let him out. His nose, ears, mouth, and eyes would become caked with clay. The clumps of clay that collected in his throat made it difficult for him to breathe. However, Mike was allowed to drink water to help flush it out.

All of the Attuans' medical records were destroyed after the war and before the American soldiers occupied Japan. However, years later, Dr. Fujino, who was the Attuans' doctor, reported that there were always ten to fifteen Attuans in intensive care at any time. In 1943, the Attuans' first year in Japan, just about everyone got sick and was taken to the hospital. They suffered from many diseases and illnesses, including tuberculosis, diphtheria, polio, beriberi, and blood poisoning.

In 1944, their second year in Japan, "Every one of us began to starve," said Mike Lokanin. He watched helplessly as his daughter, Titiana, slowly died from starvation. The very next day, his newborn son, Gabriel, starved to death. Three days later, his wife, Parascovia, was hospitalized. "It was the hardest time we had," said Mike.

Desperate for food in the winter of 1944, the

Attuan men began to hunt through the trash looking for it. Even if it was just fish heads, guts, or potato peelings, they would take it. It was what they had to do to stay alive.

"We got so hungry we would dig in the hog boxes when the guards were not looking," said Alex Prossoff. "Whatever we found we would wash it and cook it and try to eat it."

A year later, in January 1945, Chief Mike Hodikoff and his son, George, died from food poisoning after eating from the garbage. The Japanese never gave the Attuans the packages of food, clothing, and medicine that were sent by the Red Cross during the war.

"Many Attu people died in Japan," said Innokenty Golodoff. "Only twenty-five people came back."

But they didn't return to Attu. The village that they knew no longer existed. Like their boxes of bones and ashes, Attu was a casualty of war.

On the night of March 9, 1945, the United States began firebombing the cities of Japan, starting with Tokyo. Using napalm, a powder that is mixed with gasoline to create a jellylike explosive, hundreds of B-29 Superfortress planes began dropping bombs. The strategy was to attack industrial targets, factories, and railroad yards and burn down the surrounding cities.

The person in charge of the U.S. firebombing was the cigar-chomping General Curtis LeMay. He switched to the new tactic of firebombing because the high-altitude precision-bombing attacks had been ineffective in ending the war. The main obstacle had been the weather. The overcast skies and strong winds had made it difficult for the bomber pilots to hit the industrial targets.

After six firebombing raids, fifty-one square miles of Tokyo had burned to ashes, and the glow from the fire could be seen a hundred and fifty miles away. An estimated one hundred thousand Japanese died a horrific death.

When a firebomb explodes, the flaming jellylike substance from the bomb clings to and burns anything it hits. The smell of burning bodies was so intense that the bomber pilots wore oxygen masks to keep from vomiting. The massive fire also sucked the oxygen out of the air, boiled the water in the canals, and melted glass into liquid, which rolled down the streets.

The Americans relentlessly firebombed sixty-seven Japanese cities, hoping it would force the Japanese to surrender, but they refused.

On July 26, 1945, three years after Charlie and the Kiska weather team had been taken prisoners of war and three months after Benito Mussolini was executed and Hitler committed suicide, the Allies issued the Potsdam Declaration, demanding that Japan surrender unconditionally or face complete destruction. On July 28, 1945, Japan refused. The Japanese were prepared to defend their country with one million soldiers, three thousand kamikazes, five thousand suicide boats named Shinyos that were loaded with explosives and ready to crash into American ships, and millions of civilians ready and willing to fight to the death.

Nine days later, on August 6, 1945, the United States dropped an atomic bomb on Hiroshima. An estimated 140,000 people were killed, and the bomb completely devastated five square miles of the city.

Japan still refused to surrender. Two days later, on August 8, 1945, the Soviet Union declared war on Japan. The next day the United States dropped a second atomic bomb on Nagasaki.

Japan surrendered unconditionally on August 15,

1945, marking V-J Day, the Allied victory over Japan, and bringing an end to World War II.

Mushroom cloud from after the atomic bomb was dropped on Nagasaki

"I don't think I could have survived another winter as a prisoner of war in Japan," said Charlie House. "The atomic bomb saved my life, and that of the 146,000 other Allied POWs in Japan — 108,000 British and Imperial, 23,000 Dutch, and 15,000 Americans. If there had been an invasion, the Jap[anese] would have killed every one of us."

On September 2, 1945, Japan signed the surrender document, and a half an hour later there were forty-two U.S. ships and thirteen thousand troops in Tokyo Bay. The Japanese agreed to release all of the prisoners of war and accepted the authority of the U.S. supreme commander, General Douglas MacArthur. Emperor Hirohito was permitted to be

U.S. naval officers with Japanese officials at the surrender ceremony

the symbolic head of state, but he was no longer worshipped by the Japanese people.

It wasn't until the war was over that the fate of Etta Jones, the schoolteacher from Attu, was revealed. All during the war, her family tried to find out if she was alive through the Red Cross, but they never received any information.

Her family found out that Etta was, in fact, still alive, but she only weighed eighty pounds. Like all prisoners of war, she suffered from starvation. Etta had been detained with eighteen Australian nurses, and they stayed alive by stealing leftover food from the guards' plates. During their second-to-last month as prisoners, they ate almost nothing but boiled carrot greens. However, during the last two weeks the food improved when the Allied pilots dropped food parachutes.

"The Jap[anese] were really very nice to me," said Etta. "They called me the 'Oba San,' which means the 'aged one,' and is considered a title of great respect."

At sixty-five, gray-haired Etta was the oldest prisoner in the group, and the Japanese showed her more respect than they did to the younger nurses who were slapped and knocked down during their imprisonment. Some of the Australian nurses became sick with the flu, pneumonia, and beriberi. But they all survived.

All of the men from the Kiska weather team also survived their years at the Japanese prison camps. Explosion the dog survived, too.

By September 5, 1945, stories of the atrocities and brutal conditions the prisoners of war endured in Japan were published in newspapers all over the world. On that same day, the War Department issued a document directing prisoners of war not to discuss their experiences while interred or reveal any military intelligence. Walter Winfrey and other

CINCPAC-CINCPOA

5 September 1945

SUBJECT: Publicity in Connection with Liberated Prisoners of War.

1. In conformity with directive of the War Department Chief of Staff contained in dispatch WARX-55052 (031525(of 3 September 1945, which amends AG Letter 383.6 of 24 March 45, OB-S-B-M subject: Publicity Concerning Evaders, Escapers, and Prisoners of War, the following is published:

2. Released prisoners of war may release stories of their experiences after clearance with theater Bureau of Public Relations headquarters or War Department Bureau of Public Relations with the following exceptions:

(a) There will not be published in any form whatsoever, or either directly or indirectly communicated to press, radio or any persons except to representatives of the appropriate theater intelligence section, as designated by theater commanders or to American military attaches or to the AC of G-2, WDGS any details or references concerning the following:

(1) Unannounced organizations which have assisted evaders and escapers or methods used by these organizations.

(2) Any means of identifying helpers, such as names, pictures, descriptions, etc.

(3) Evasion and Escape equipment and special intelligence activities within the prison camps.

3. Commanding officers will be responsible for instructing all subject personnel in the provisions of this directive, and insuring that the attached certificate be executed.

SECURITY CERTIFICATE

I certify that I have read and fully understand all the provisions of the Directive of the Secretary of War as is printed on this sheet, and will at ALL TIMES hereafter comply fully therewith.

I understand that disclosure of secret military information to unauthorized persons will make me liable to disciplinary action for failure to safeguard such information.

I realize that it is my duty during my military service, and later as a civilian, to take all possible precautions to prevent disclosure, by word of mouth or otherwise, of military information of this nature.

Name (print)_____ Signed_____

Rank_____ A.S.N._____ Date_____ Place_____

Unit_____ Witness_____

Document issued by the U.S. government for POWs to sign, directing them not discuss their experiences

prisoners signed the document, promising to keep the information secret. They and many other POWs didn't want to talk about their experiences because it was too painful. They wanted nothing more than to forget about what had happened to them.

World War II was over, and with it the Aleutian War. Years later, it would be referred to as the Forgotten War because many Americans forgot or never knew that the Japanese invaded Alaska. It would be decades before these unforgettable stories were told.

Walter Winfrey one year after his return from Japan as a POW

AFTERWORD
The Remembered

ATONEMENT

Between July 1981 and December 1982 the Commission on Wartime Relocation and Internment of Civilians launched an investigation into the five Aleut evacuee camps. The Commission condemned the U.S. government for its "indifference" to the "deplorable conditions" at the evacuee camps.

On August 10, 1988, President Ronald Reagan signed the Civil Liberties Act, a reparations law for the Aleuts and the Japanese Americans who were interned during World War II. The Aleuts received restitution from the government for their suffering and losses that included a 5-million-dollar trust fund for the Aleuts, 15 million dollars for the loss of Attu Island, 1.4 million dollars for the restoration of church properties, and individual payments of 12,000 dollars to each Aleut who survived the camps.

The Aleuts were also issued a formal apology from the U.S. government.

PEACE

In the United States, the Japanese invasion and occupation of the Aleutians is often called the Forgotten War. But in Japan, no one has forgotten it. Every year the Japanese celebrate the lives of the soldiers who fought and died in the Aleutians.

In June 1987, with the cooperation of the U.S. government, Japan placed a peace monument on Attu Island. The towering nineteen-foot monument states, in both English and Japanese, "IN MEMORY OF ALL THOSE WHO SACRIFICED THEIR LIVES IN THE ISLANDS AND SEAS OF THE NORTH PACIFIC DURING WORLD WAR II AND IN DEDICATION TO WORLD PEACE."

FRIENDS

In 1985, Sherman Smith wrote a letter to Dr. Yasuo Sassa, president of the Japanese Alpine Club. In his letter, Sherman told Dr. Sassa about a Japanese flag he had found on Kiska Island forty-two years earlier while serving with the army's Eighty-Seventh Mountain Infantry, Tenth Division. Sherman recently had the names on the flag translated from the Japanese characters into English, and he asked Dr. Sassa if he knew whether Mr. Kasukabe, whose name was on the flag, was still alive.

Karl Kasukabe was, in fact, still alive. Now

seventy-two, he'd lived the long life he'd hoped for. Sherman's letter was forwarded to Karl, and he wrote back immediately, saying he was "surprised and moved."

Later that year, Sherman traveled to Japan to return the flag to Karl Kasukabe, and an unexpected friendship developed.

In 1993, the Eighty-Seventh Mountain Infantry, Tenth Division, held a fifty-year reunion on Kiska to share memories and honor the dead. Karl was invited to attend. During the reunion, they held a joint Christian-Buddhist memorial ceremony with sake and rice cakes.

"We thought we would die here," said Karl. "But to survive and come back is something I would never have thought. My spirit soars."

Karl, who walked with the help of a cane due to his injuries from the Kiska bombing, summed it up: "Enemies fifty years ago, now dear friends."

Acknowledgments

I owe thanks to many people. First, I want to thank Jessica Regel and Brenda Murray, whose conversation at a lunch meeting led to the topic of the Aleutian War — and now you know the rest of the story.

Many thanks are also due to Alice Juda at the Naval War College. Alice tenaciously tracked down Charlie House's nineteen-page report on surviving in the Kiska wilderness. She also connected me with Don Cruse, who put me in touch with his lifelong friend, Walter Winfrey.

At the time of this writing, Walter had just celebrated his ninety-fifth birthday. His eyesight is not what it used to be nor is his hearing, but he graciously answered all of my questions — unless, of course, the answers were still classified. When he was asked what was top secret about the antennas they were installing on Kiska and if they had something to do with the emerging radar technology, he wouldn't say. He just smiled.

Walter has never before spoken about his painful experience as a POW, and the fact that the interview happened at all is because of his daughter, Wanona Carey. She took my questions to her dad and wrote out all of his answers for me. Thank you.

It was also through my contact with Don Cruse and Alice Juda that I heard from Barbara Envison, Charlie House's daughter. Somehow a letter I sent in the mail with an old address Don had given me found its way to Barbara, and she called me as soon as she received it. Not only was she a pleasure to talk to, but Barbara answered all of my questions about her dad, for which I am very grateful.

Alice Juda also led me to Janis Kozlowski of the National Park Service in Anchorage, Alaska. Janis generously provided me with a copy of Paul Carrigan's memoirs, a photo of the Kiska Weather Team, and transcribed interviews of Simeon Pletnikoff, the heroic Aleut Pete.

Dennis Hagen of the Denver Public Library Western History and Genealogy Department made my day when he helped me find detailed background information about Karl Kaoru Kasukabe. The information revealed that Karl was, in fact, the interpreter on Attu whom Mike Lokanin remembered, as well as being the owner of the booby-trapped Japanese flag that Sherman Smith found on Kiska.

Dawn Harrison at the Alaska Medical Library was a great help in providing me with many articles on everything from the invasion of Attu to Castner's Cutthroats.

I also wish to thank Millie McKeown and Sharon Kay of the Aleutian Pribilof Islands Association, Kathleen Shoemaker of Emory University, Eileen Kakazu of the School of Medicine at Loma Linda University, and Lainey Cronk of Pacific Union College.

Special thanks to my husband, Todd, whose encouraging words helped me every step of the way.

Source Notes

"18 Australian Women Freed in Yokohama." *Argus* (Melbourne, Australia), September 3, 1945.

"Alaska Fur Farmer Has Good Crop of Foxes." *Fur News and Outdoor World*, October 1920, reprinted in *Fur-Fish-Game*, vols. 31–32, p. 11. Columbus: A. R. Harding Publishing Co., 1920.

"Annual Report of the United States Revenue-Cutter Service for the Fiscal Year Ended June 30, 1914." Washington, DC: Government Printing Office, 1914, p. 186.

"Japanese Erect a Monument to Those Who Died on Attu." *Ellensburg Daily Record* (Ellensburg, WA), June 22, 1987.

"Paul Tatsuguchi: Even His Name Will Die." *The Journal of Ethnic Studies*, 3 (Winter 1976), pp. 37–48 and interview transcript of Mrs. Tatsuguchi. Floyd Watkins' Collection. Manuscript, Archives, and Rare Book Library (MARBL), Emory University.

Aleut Evacuation: The Untold War Story. DVD. Directed by Michael and Mary Jo Thill. Girdwood, AK: Gaff Rigged Productions for the Aleutian Pribilof Islands Association. 1992.

Azzole, Pete. "Afterthoughts: Rochefort on: The Battle of Midway — June 1942." *Cryptolog*, 1995.

——. "Afterthoughts: Rochefort on: The Making of a 'Cryppy.'" *Cryptolog*, 1995.

——. "Afterthoughts: Rochefort on: The Second Japanese Attack on Pearl Harbor." *Cryptolog*, 1995.

——. "Afterthoughts: Rochefort on: Smoking Jackets, Felt Slippers and Cryptanalysis." *Cryptolog*, 1995.

——. "Afterthoughts: Rochefort on: A Successful Failure; Communications Intelligence and Pearl Harbor." *Cryptolog*, 1995.

Bank, Theodore P., et al. "We Left Our Village Burning." *The University of Michigan Expedition to the Aleutians, 1948–49.* Unpublished preliminary report to the Office of Naval Research, Department of the Navy, pp. 31–35.

Bartholomew, Frank. "Brutality, Filth, Pathos — Prison Stories Unfold." *Eugene Register-Guard*, August 31, 1945.

Berreman, Gerald D. "Effects of a Technological Change in an Aleutian Village." *Arctic*, vol. 7, no. 2, 1954, pp. 102–107.

Breu, Mary. *Last Letters from Attu: The True Story of Etta Jones, Alaska Pioneer and Japanese P.O.W.* Portland, OR: Alaska Northwest Books, 2009.

Brice, Howard. "Etta Jones . . . P.O.W." *Alaska Life*, December 1945.

Budiansky, Stephen. *Battle of Wits: The Complete Story of Codebreaking in World War II.* New York: Free Press, 2000.

——. "Codebreaking with IBM Machines in World War II." *Cryptologia*, October 2001.

Byas, Hugh. "Japan Draws the Map of a Vast 'Lebensraum.'" *New York Times*, February 2, 1941.

Carrigan, Paul E. *The Flying, Fighting Weathermen of Patrol Wing Four: 1941–1945.* Forked River, NJ: Regal-Lith Printers, 2002.

Chandonnet, Fern, ed. *Alaska at War, 1941–1945: The Forgotten War Remembered*. Fairbanks: University of Alaska Press, 2007. Republished from *Alaska at War, 1941–1945: The Forgotten War Remembered: Papers from the Alaska War Symposium*, Anchorage, AK, November 11–13, 1993.

Chicago Daily Tribune. "Attu Mystery: What Happened to 45 Indians?" August 8, 1943.

——. "Ensign's Dog Welcomes Him Back to Kiska." August 31, 1943.

——. "Revealed Sad Fate of Attu's Only White Couple." July 28, 1944.

——. "Tell How Jap Women Mauled Yankee Flyers." September 2, 1945.

——. "Woman, 65, Attu Teacher, Kicked Beaten by Japs." September 13, 1945.

Chihaya, Masataka. "The Withdrawal from Kiska." In *The Japanese Navy in World War II*, edited by David C. Evans. Annapolis: U.S. Naval Institute, 1969.

Cloe, John. *The Aleutian Warriors: A History of the 11th Air Force & Fleet Air Wing Four*. Anchorage Chapter — Air Force Association and Pictorial Histories Publishing Company, Inc. 1991.

Codebreakers. VHS. Written by William Woolard and Brian Johnson; directed by Brian Johnson. Boston, MA: A NOVA production by inCA Ltd. for WGBH/Boston in association with NDR International, 1994.

Driscoll, Joseph. *War Discovers Alaska*. Philadelphia: Lippincott, 1943.

Duncan, Gordon. "Record Seal Catch." *Wall Street Journal*, September 29, 1943.

Durdin, F. Tillman. "All Captives Slain." *New York Times*, December 18, 1937.

Eddy, Don. "Tough Guy Holds Alaska." *Los Angeles Times*, January 31, 1943.

Erickson, Leif. "Japs May Have Fled Aleutians to Escape the Colonel's Jibe." *Palm Beach Post*, November 7, 1943.

——. "Pacific Storms Work for Japs; But Weather Sometimes Crosses Up Foe by Exposing Convoys." *Lewiston Evening Journal* (Lewiston, ME), June 18, 1943.

——. "What It Means Told of Tokyo after Bombing." *Sarasota Herald-Tribune*, May 30, 1945.

Fankhauser, Jill. "Alaska Scouts Reunite." *Alaska Star*, October 9, 2008. http://www.alaskastar.com/stories/100908/new_20081009002 .shtml.

Feuer, A. B. *Packs On! Memoirs of the 10th Mountain Division in WWII*. Westport, CT: Praeger Publishers, 2004; reissued Mechanicsburg, PA: Stackpole Books, 2006 (paperback).

Ford, Corey. *Shortcut to Tokyo: The Battle for the Aleutians*. New York: Scribner's, 1943.

Fosdick, Dean. "Aleutian Veterans Return to Kiska — Former Enemies Share Memories, Honor Dead." *Seattle Times*, September 19, 1993.

Frisbee, John L. "Valor: Eareckson on the Aleutians." *Air Force Magazine*, vol. 74, no. 6, June 1991.

Garfield, Brian. *The Thousand-Mile War: World War II in Alaska and the Aleutians*. Fairbanks: University of Alaska Press, 1969; reissued 1995 (paperback).

Golodoff, Innokenty. "Last Days of Attu Village." Translated by Karl W. Kenyon. *Alaska Sportsman*, December 1966.

Gray, George. "George Gray — Cutthroat." *Alaska Life: The Territorial Magazine*, vol. 8, April 1945, pp. 19–31, 58–60.

Hailey, Foster. "Evacuation Tactic at Kiska Is Puzzle." *New York Times*, August 22, 1943.

———. "Japanese on Kiska Lived in Cave and Sod Houses of Crude Village." *New York Times*, August 24, 1943.

Hall, Jim. "The Battle for Attu." *DAV*, May–June 2003.

Halpin, James. "Stealth Fighters Ghosted through Aleutian Campaign." *Anchorage Daily News*, September 28, 2008.

Hamilton, Andrew J. "Science Pins Down the Weather." *Popular Mechanics*, vol. 85, no. 2, February 1946, p. 40.

Handleman, Howard. "13 Captured Japs on Attu Beg to Work for America." *Reading Eagle* (Reading, PA), June 19, 1943.

Harding, Stephen. "What We Learned . . . from the Battle of Attu." *Military History*, Feb/Mar 2009.

Haugland, Vern. "Airmen Tell of Jap Brutality at Torture Camp." *Los Angeles Times*, September 1, 1945.

Hays, Otis. *Alaska's Hidden Wars: Secret Campaigns on the North Pacific Rim*. Fairbanks: University of Alaska Press, 2004.

Holmes, W. J. *Double-Edged Secrets: U.S. Naval Operations in the Pacific During World War II*. Annapolis, MD: U.S. Naval Institute Press, 1979; reissued 1998 (paperback).

Horiki, Hiroshi. "The Mystery of Kiska Island Evacuation."
Nippon Keizai Shimbun (Japan Economy Newspaper), August 15,
1985. Sherman L. Smith Papers, The Denver Public Library —
Western History/Genealogy Department.

House, William Charles. Report to Neil F. O'Connor, USN, College
of Naval Warfare, Newport, RI. Postwar. Not dated.

——. "Reunion between William C. House, Steve Hodikoff,
Innokenty and Willie Golodoff, May 20, 1979." Letter to the
Commission on Wartime Relocation and Internment of Civilians
dated January 21, 1982. Copy from the National Archives.

Hughes, Alice. "A Woman's New York." *Reading Eagle* (Reading,
PA), August 9, 1949.

Hurd, Charles. "15 Tons of Bombs Dropped On Japanese Base at
Kiska." *New York Times*, October 10, 1942.

——. "Claim Is Scouted." *New York Times*, June 11, 1942.

Johnson, Hal. "So We're Told." *Berkeley Daily Gazette*, March 7, 1944.

Jones, Etta. "I Am the Woman the Japs Captured in the Aleutians."
Pacific Motor Boat, September 1946.

Jordan, David Starr. "Colonial Lessons of Alaska." *Atlantic
Monthly*, vol. 82, November 1898, 577–591.

Kasukabe, Karl Kaoru to R. James Mockford. June 10, 1985.
Sherman L. Smith Papers, The Denver Public Library — Western
History/Genealogy Department.

Kirkland, John C., and David Coffin, Jr. *The Relocation and
Internment of the Aleuts During World War II*, vols. 1–8. Anchorage:
Aleutian Pribilof Islands Association: 1981. CD-ROM.

Kluckhohn, Frank L. "Serious Setback." *New York Times*, December 10, 1941.

Kohlhoff, Dean. *When the Wind Was a River: Aleut Evacuation in World War II*. Seattle: University of Washington Press (in association with Aleutian Pribilof Islands Association, Anchorage), 1995.

Lantis, Margaret. "Aleut." *Handbook of North American Indians*, vol. 5. Washington, DC: Smithsonian Institution, 1984.

Larrabee, Eric. *Commander in Chief: Franklin Delano Roosevelt, His Lieutenants, and Their War*. Annapolis, MD: U.S. Naval Institute Press, 2004.

Layton, Rear Admiral Edwin T., USN (Ret.). *"And I Was There": Pearl Harbor and Midway — Breaking the Secrets*. With Capt. Roger Pineau, USNR (Ret.), and John Costello. New York: William Morrow, 1985; reissued Annapolis, MD: U.S. Naval Institute Press, 2006 (paperback).

Long, Levi J. "WWII Internments Set Aleuts Adrift from their Islands." *Seattle Times*, February 19, 2004.

Lord, Walter. *Incredible Victory*. Harper & Row, 1967; reissued as *Incredible Victory: The Battle of Midway*. Springfield, NJ: Burford Books, 1998 (paperback).

Los Angeles Times. "Japan Faces Shortage in its Food Supply." December 22, 1939.

——. "Japs Menace to West Coast Told Senators." April 17, 1943.

——. "Japs Slew Own Patients on Attu, Diary Discloses." September 10, 1943.

——. "Refugees Tell of Aleutian Raids." July 15, 1942.

——. "Sadistic Medical Tortures Related by Freed Yanks." September 2, 1945.

Loughlin, John. "War Prisoners Tell of Horrors of Japanese Camps." *Canberra Times*, September 3, 1945.

Mariner, M. A. "Aleut Priest Hopes to Right Internment Camp Wrongs." *Anchorage Daily News*, July 14, 1981.

Marshall, Jim. "Fateful Aleutians." Review of *Short Cut to Tokyo: The Battle for the Aleutians*, by Corey Ford. *New York Times*, May 9, 1943.

Martin, Russell. "The Optical Aleutian." *American History Illustrated*, vol. 33, no. 1, March 1988.

McDaniel, Sandi. "Of Time and the Island a Gathering of Old Enemies Tries to Allay One of the Bloodiest Battles of the Pacific." *Anchorage Daily News*, July 11, 1993.

——. "On Display: Artists' View of Aleutians at War." *Anchorage Daily News*, November 7, 1993.

——. "Searching for a Father on Attu for Daughter of WWII Japanese Medic, Island Is Link to a Parent She Never Knew." *Anchorage Daily News*, July 16, 1993.

McDowell, Edwin. "Officer Who Broke Japanese War Codes Gets Belated Honor." *New York Times*, November 17, 1985.

McQuaid, B. J. "Air Power to Crush Japs in Aleutians Growing." *Los Angeles Times*, November 12, 1942.

——. "Giant Bomber Raid on Kiska Described." *Los Angeles Times*, November 9, 1942.

——. "Raiders of Kiska Row Over Who'll Kill Japs." *Los Angeles Times*, November 13, 1942.

Meyer, Jeremy. "Soldiers with an Altitude." *Yakima Herald-Republic*, October 18, 1998.

Meyers, Georg N. "The Alaska Scouts." *The Best From Yank the Army Weekly*. New York: E. P. Dutton, 1945, pp. 190–193.

Milwaukee Journal. "Catalina, Built for Long-Range Patrol, Stars as Fighter, Torpedo, Dive Bomber." April 7, 1943.

Mitchell, Lt. Robert J., compiler. *The Capture of Attu: A World War II Battle as Told by the Men Who Fought There.* With Sewell T. Tyng and Capt. Nelson L. Drummond Jr. Lincoln: University of Nebraska Press, 2000.

Morgan, Lael, ed. *The Aleutians.* Anchorage: The Alaska Geographical Society, 1980.

Naval Aviation News. "Patwing 4 over the Aleutians." February 1943.

New York Times. "Eyewitness Extols Navy Raids on Kiska." July 15, 1942.

——. "Japan on American Soil." July 22, 1942.

——. "Japan's Economy Held Weakening." April 4, 1940.

——. "Japanese Explain Kiska Evacuation." August 22, 1943.

——. "Japanese on Kiska Report U.S. Raids." July 25, 1942.

——. "Joint Task Forces to Free Prisoners." September 3, 1945.

——. "Navy Weatherman Has Troubles, Too." August 11, 1949.

——. "Pre-War Axis Plan Aimed at Alaska." June 7, 1942

——. "Tokyo, Reporting Kiska-Attu Seizure, Claims Thrust Into Near-By Islands." June 26, 1942.

Nutchuk. *Back to the Smoky Sea*. With Alan Hatch. New York: J. Messner, Inc., 1946.

O'Connor, James. "More Evidence of Jap Brutality: Interviews with POWs in Hospital Ship." *Argus* (Melbourne), September 5, 1945.

O'Harra, Doug. "Hallowed Ground Military and Native Leaders Return to Attu to Remember and Learn." *Anchorage Daily News*, June 29, 1997.

Oliver, Ethel Ross. *Journal of an Aleutian Year*. Seattle: University of Washington Press, 1988.

Pearl Harbor: December 7, 1941. DVD, commemorative edition. Disc 2. "Recognition of a Japanese Zero Fighter." Directed by John Ford. St. Laurent, Quebec, Canada: Madacy Entertainment, 2001.

Perala, Andrew. "Retired Admiral Recalls Cold War in Aleutians." *Anchorage Daily News*, October 9, 1985.

Prokopeuff, Olean (Golodoff). "An Account of the WWII Attu Captivity." Excerpt from *The Aleutian Invasion* by Ray Hudson and Unalaska High School students. 1981. http://www.hlswilliwaw.com/aleutians/attu/html/attu_account_of-attu_captivity.htm

Rall, Mary M. "Alaska Scouts Capture Focus of Anchorage Museum Display." *Alaska Post*, October 3, 2008.

Rearden, Jim. *Forgotten Warriors of the Aleutian Campaign*. Missoula, MT: Pictorial Histories Publishing Company, Inc., 2005.

Reese, Lee Fleming. "The Truth about Pearl Harbor." *San Diego Union*, April 2, 1989.

Rempel, William C. "One Helluva Existence." *Los Angeles Times*, August 9, 1976.

Report from the Aleutians. Short format film. Written, directed, and narrated (with Walter Huston) by John Huston. Produced by the Army Signal Corps and released by the U.S. War Department, August 1943. Viewable at http://www.archive.org/details/ReportFromTheAleutians.

Rubin, Julia. "Alaska's Aleuts — Forgotten Internees of WWII Captivity." *Los Angeles Times*, March 1, 1992.

Salvatore, Susan Cianci. *Civil Rights in America: Racial Voting Rights — A National Historic Landmarks Theme Study*. Washington, DC: U.S. Department of the Interior, National Park Service, 2009.

Shalett, Sidney. "Island Evacuated." *New York Times*, August 22, 1943.

——. "Skip-Bomb Secret Revealed by Army." *New York Times*, June 24, 1943.

Sherman L. Smith Papers. Denver Public Library: Western History and Genealogy.

Smith, Michael. *The Emperor's Codes: The Breaking of Japan's Secret Ciphers*. New York: Arcade Publishing, 2001; reissued 2007 (paperback).

Smith, Sherman L. "Roots, Brief Personal History of the Kasukabes." Sherman L. Smith Papers. Denver Public Library: Western History and Genealogy.

St. George Seal Skin Plant Pribilof Islands. National Park Service brochure. *www.stgeorgealaska.com/seal_skin_plant.pdf.*

St. Petersburg Times. "Woman, Captured on Attu, Freed." September 3, 1945.

Stevens, Kathie. "Eagles Thick as Crows in Alaskan Scenery." *Knoxville News-Sentinel,* March, 20, 2001, sec. B.

Sydney Morning Herald. "Ghosts Fight Allies." February 2, 1944.

Symonds, Craig L. *Decision at Sea: Five Naval Battles that Shaped American History.* New York: Oxford University Press, 2005 (hardcover); reissued 2006 (paperback).

Theodore Bank Collection. University of Alaska Anchorage.

Time. "Army & Navy — Operations: Tundra Troopers." August 9, 1943.

———. "World Battlefronts: Battle of Alaska: Under Cover." July 6, 1942.

Tominga, Takaki. "Postwar60: Japanese widow remembers husband killed in Battle of Attu." *Asian Political News,* August 15, 2005.

Turner, James Leroy. "The Attack on Kiska Island." A report written for Admiral James Russell. Postwar. Not dated.

Unalaska High School students. *Cuttlefish Volumes One, Two & Three: Stories of Aleutian Culture & History.* Unalaska, AK: Unalaska City School, 1977–79.

United States Commission on Wartime Relocation and Internment of Civilians. *Personal Justice Denied.* Seattle: University of Washington Press, 1996.

Van de Water, Marjorie. "How To Spot Airplanes." *Science News Letter*, January 31, 1942, p. 70.

Van Ells, Mark. "Jim O'Dair." *Wisconsin Stories*. Wisconsin Veterans Museum, December 1997. http://wisconsinstories.org.

Weadon, Patrick D. "How Cryptology Enabled the United States to Turn the Tide in the Pacific War." *The Course to Midway*. Department of the Navy website: http://www.navy.mil/midway/how.html.

Wheeler, Keith. "Big Jap Force Dealt Blow in Aleutian Fog." *Los Angeles Times*, July 19, 1942.

——. "Catalina Flying Boats Get Valiant Help From Tender." *Toledo Blade*, July 24, 1942.

——. "Catalinas Halted Aleutian Invader." *New York Times*, July 22, 1942.

——. "Hazards of Bombing Attacks on Japs at Kiska Described by Newsman Who Saw Show." *Los Angeles Times*, July 26, 1942.

——. "Kiska May Prove Tomb of Jap Hopes." *Los Angeles Times*, July 21, 1942.

——. *The Pacific Is My Beat*. New York: E. P. Dutton, 1943.

Winfrey, Walter Monroe. "Aleutian Attack of 7 June 1942." A report written for Admiral James Russell. Dated December 14, 1946.

Yeo, Henry K. "Tatsy: Rendezvous at Attu. Aftermath." Loma Linda University School of Medicine Alumni Journal, vol. 64, no. 2.

Yeo, Henry, and Heather Reifsnyder. "Same Family, Different Sides." *SCOPE*, Spring 2007.

Image Credits

Page 9 top & bottom: USNI [United States Naval Institute]; page 11: Corry Station Museum/U.S. Naval Cryptologic Veterans Association; page 12: Time & Life Pictures/Getty Images; page 15: USNI [United States Naval Institute]; page 19: Corry Station Museum/U.S. Naval Cryptologic Veterans Association; page 23: map by James McMahon/ Scholastic NY; pages 25, 27: UAA/APU Consortium Library/University of Alaska, Anchorage; page 29: University Images Group Limited/ Alamy; page 31: Alaska State Library; page 32: UAA/APU Consortium Library/University of Alaska, Anchorage; pages 34 left & right, 35: Elmer E. Rashmuson Library/University of Alaska, Fairbanks; page 48: U.S. geological survey by Amar Andalkar; page 50: Alaska State Library; page 54: National Archives; pages 63, 68, 70, 73, 76, 79, 89: Alaska State Library; page 90: National Archives; page 92: courtesy of Barbara House Envison; page 104: Elmer E. Rashmuson Library/ University of Alaska, Fairbanks; pages 108, 110: Alaska State Library; page 112: Alaska Veterans Museum Project; pages 114, 116: Alaska State Library; pages 117, 120: Elmer E. Rashmuson Library/University of Alaska, Fairbanks; page 122: Alaska State Library; pages 125, 126: Elmer E. Rashmuson Library/University of Alaska, Fairbanks; page 128: Alaska State Library; page 129: Elmer E. Rashmuson Library/ University of Alaska, Fairbanks; page 133: Anchorage Museum; page 139: Elmer E. Rashmuson Library/University of Alaska, Fairbanks; pages 141, 144, 145, 148, 153, 155: Alaska State Library; page 159: Elmer E. Rashmuson Library/University of Alaska, Fairbanks; pages 163, 165, 172, 176, 184: Alaska State Library; page 189: Associated Press; page 190: Alaska State Library; pages 192, 193: courtesy of Wanona Carey.

Index

Page numbers in boldface refer to images.

B

C

217